THE SAFARI PRESS LIMITED EDITION COLLECTION

1985–2005

The trademark Safari Press ® is registered with the U.S. Patent and Trademark Office and in other countries.

Safari Press

First edition

Safari Press Inc.

2006, Long Beach, California

ISBN 1-57157-229-5

Library of Congress Catalog Card Number: 2005926569

10 9 8 7 6 5 4 3 2 1

Printed in Singapore

Readers wishing to receive the Safari Press catalog, featuring many fine books on big-game hunting, wingshooting, and sporting firearms, should write to Safari Press Inc., P.O. Box 3095, Long Beach, CA 90803, USA. Tel: (714) 894-9080 or visit our Web site at www.safaripress.com.

Table of Contents

* SOLD OUT. LISTS ORIGINAL ISSUE PRICE.

SAFARI PRESS

THE LIMITED EDITION COLLECTION

Safari Press 1985–2005

Welcome to Safari Press and its limited edition series. This brochure is not a catalog of books for sale. As you will see, over half the books listed in these pages are (long since) sold out, and we have no copies to offer. The purpose of this brochure is to provide a complete bibliographical work of all the Safari Press limited edition books we have published up until early 2005.

We decided to bring out this brochure to mark our twentieth anniversary . . . a milestone for us at Safari Press and an accomplishment for which we are justifiably proud. Many thousands of businesses get started each week in the United States, and most, if we are to believe the statistics, do not make it to year three. Starting from very meager beginnings in a small garage of a townhouse, we have grown to a company that occupies thousands of square feet of offices and warehouse space and has some seventeen employees. All this is not the vision or work of one individual but rather the cumulative efforts of all the people who work for Safari Press. Equally, or even more importantly, it is the cumulative efforts of the dozens and dozens of authors, artists, and photographers who have produced the raw product that we forged into books.

In May 1984 we issued a small, dark green catalog under the name World Wide Hunting Books. The logo was that of a white rhino on a shield. World Wide Hunting Books sold (and still does) antiquarian big-game hunting books by issuing a catalog about four times a year. In 1985 we published our first book, which was a reprint by James Mellon entitled *African Hunter*. We adopted the name Safari Press and used the rhino logo from WWHB. From this small beginning, the company has grown till today when we have published over two hundred titles and printed nearly a million copies of our books. We started the business in Seal Beach, California, and we remained there until 1990 when we moved to a commercial office and warehouse in Huntington Beach. Initially we occupied one unit in a building, but over time, thanks to a landlord who was kind and a sportsman to boot, we came to occupy the entire building. The emphasis of the press was African big-game hunting from the outset, but soon we published our first sporting-firearms book by Craig Boddington entitled *Safari Rifles*. From there we branched out to wingshooting, North American and Asian big game, and mountain hunting.

Safari Press has grown exponentially from its inception, and we believe that the strength of the press has been to stick with what we know. From the beginning, we had writers and editors who understood narrative for big-game hunting, sporting firearms, and wingshooting. We, by and large, stayed away from how-to hunting books and published books on deer hunting sparingly. It is not that we lacked expertise in these areas or that the subject matter was not worthwhile. We simply felt that how-to and deer-hunting books were so well covered by other publishing companies that we needed to pursue other opportunities.

As we have reached our first major milestone, we felt it was time to reflect on what we've accomplished over two decades. As you look through these pages, you can see that we have produced many different titles. You will also note that this brochure contains only our limited edition books, virtually all of them slipcased and signed by the author. As you probably know, we have also produced many other books that we chose to designate as "trade editions." These never showed up as limited edition books, and, therefore, fall outside the scope of this brochure. And, of course, many of our limited edition books, once sold out, have been reprinted in trade editions, normally in the form of a hardcover book with a dust jacket.

Let's say a word about the trade books that have never been published in a limited edition. There is, of course, irony in the fact that several of our all-time best sellers in both units sold and dollars generated were never issued as limited editions. There is good reason for this: They were simply never suitable to be limited editions. Take *Ammo & Ballistics* by Robert Forker for instance. The book has seen numerous printings, and

the third edition will be released in 2006. It was never even issued in a hardcover; from day one it was a softcover book. Are we glad we published it? Absolutely, but to have issued this book in a limited edition as a collector's item would have bordered on effrontery.

Our limited editions are, for the most part, books that tell a story. They seldom offer practical shooting or ballistic information, and they don't discuss how-to hunting tactics. We purposely choose the titles for each limited edition series based on this rationale. Our limited editions series are a reflection of hunting and sporting firearms as it is and was in the twentieth and the twenty-first centuries.

In the high country subsistence farms perch precariously on benches and terraces. The Ethiopian people are hard-working and admirable—but human encroachment and deforestation for firewood are the mountain nyala's greatest enemies

My March 2000 mountain nyala is a superb trophy and one that I didn't think possible until Negussie got the new area. This nyala was taken with a single 220-grain Sierra from my 8mm Remington Magnum.

We are particularly pleased to tell you that Safari Press has now produced more original, limited edition titles than either Amwell Press or the original Derrydale Press. The truth of the matter is that a publishing company has a very hard time making a living off publishing limited edition books alone. The last one hundred years has seen various American sporting publishers struggle and, sadly, also fail by publishing limited editions only. Safari Press's strategy from the beginning has been to publish both limited- and trade-edition books. It has been a good mix for the company.

With the exception of three books—*White Hunter* by John Hunter, *Horned Death* by John Burger, and *After Big Game in Central Africa* by Edouard Foa—all our limited edition books have been original titles not published before in the English language. All our limited edition books are numbered and most have been signed by the author(s). Virtually all limited edition books were issued with a slipcase. We have taken particular care in working with the very best slipcase makers we could find. In the very beginning we issued a few books with paper-covered slipcases. It was apparent within a year that these slipcases would not stand the test of time; hence, we switched over to slipcases that are covered with wax-impregnated linen and "vellum"cloth. These are twice as expensive to make as paper-covered slipcases, but the results speak for themselves.

When we publish an original title in a limited edition only, that limited edition is the only first edition for that title. This has kept the number of true first-edition Safari Press books very small, a fact that has reached the consciousness of the reader and collector. There is considerable variation in the use of the term "first edition" in the book-collecting world. However, a widely accepted definition by *The Chicago Manual of Style* holds that, if a book is reprinted with a substantially different binding or price or the text is markedly altered, then one can fairly describe such a book as a new edition. Since we issue our limited editions in a format very much different from that of our trade editions, it is correct to refer to our limited editions as "first editions," which is what we have chosen to do.

Inevitably when writing an essay like this, one is apt to ponder the future. Safari Press will continue to publish limited edition books, but we will also continue to adapt and expand our publishing program to keep up with the times. This year will see our first audio books in production, and we have now published two books that are available for download from the Internet as well as in printed format. As many of our customers know, we have purchased a magazine—*Sports Afield,* no less—and we see ourselves continuing to expand a variety of products that cater to the hunter and sporting-firearm enthusiast. However, the core of Safari Press shall remain its limited editions. The most famous people in the hunting world have contributed to these series—Prince Abdorreza, Craig Boddington, Peter H. Capstick, Robin Hurt, and Tony Sanchez-Ariño, just to name a few. Our promise is to continue to seek out and then produce the very best there is in hunting literature for our reading public.

Ludo Wurfbain, *Publisher*
Dr. Jacqueline Neufeld, *Editor in Chief*
January 2005

Classics in African Hunting Series

THE SAFARI PRESS LIMITED EDITION COLLECTION

Classics in African Hunting Series

This series, which we launched in 1986, is devoted exclusively to books on African big-game hunting. The series now has well over fifty titles in it, which makes it larger than any other series of African hunting books ever published. As we said in the general introduction, only three of our African books have been reprints; all the others are original titles. With fifty-some-odd books, it is hard to pick out any favorites to discuss in this overview, so we will just mention a few of these books and relate some interesting anecdotes about them.

From Mt. Kenya to the Cape (1987) was our first original title and Craig Boddington's first African hunting book. I can recall sitting with Craig in his home in Los Angeles going over the particulars of the contract and resisting publishing the book! Craig wanted it out right then, but I wanted to wait till Craig had come back from his proposed mountain nyala hunt so as to include that episode in the book. In the end Craig won, and it was a good thing, too, because the mountain nyala hunt turned out to be years, not weeks, away.

A few years later, we published *Safari Rifles* (1990), also by Craig Boddington. It should have been in Safari Press's Classics in Sporting Firearms Series; however, we did not launch that series until 1995, so we placed Craig's second book in the Classics in African Hunting Series, not realizing at the time that we would ever do a firearms series. Here's how *Safari Rifles* came to be: Craig had come up with the idea of the *Mt. Kenya* book, and a year or so later we decided that we had better come up with a vision for another African book for Craig, given the immense popularity of his writings. We hit upon the idea of doing a new, updated version of John Taylor's classic *African Rifles and Cartridges,* and we asked Craig to write it. He did a masterful job of writing *Safari Rifles,* and this title turned out to be his all-time bestselling book. After nearly fifteen years and many print runs later, it still is in print.

We did a limited edition of only 500 copies, and it is one of the few books we bound in leather.

In 1992 we launched a series within a series with the "African Country Series." This series, which would ultimately contain eight volumes, was a compilation of hunting stories from each country, arranged in chronological order. Tony Sanchez-Ariño was the general editor for the series, and we commissioned various artists—those who had lived or were from the country—to do original artwork for each volume. The first volume in this series was *Hunting in Tanzania,* followed by Zimbabwe, Sudan, Botswana, Ethiopia, Zambia, South Africa, and Kenya. We issued the first three volumes in this series (Tanzania, Zimbabwe, and Sudan) at $125 each, and all others came out at $135. Tanzania and Zimbabwe have long since sold out, and they bring the highest aftermarket prices of any out-of-print Safari Press book. Repeatedly in the last few years, copies of *Hunting in Tanzania* have fetched prices of $700 to $800, selling very quickly once offered.

Peter Capstick is a well-known name to all in the hunting world, and were we ever happy to hear from his agent in New York when he wanted to find a publisher for *A Man Called Lion.* We had known Peter for a number of years and cooperated with him on the distribution of his books and videos, and I remember staying at Fiona and Peter Capstick's house in South Africa and enjoying a delicious meal of frog legs in a local restaurant. Based on research by Brian Marsh, *A Man Called Lion* tells the life story of the controversial character John "Pondoro" Taylor. This book is the last book Peter wrote and signed in a limited edition; in fact, this is the *only* book Peter Capstick wrote that he also signed as a limited *first* edition.

Through Brian Marsh, I met Ian Nyschens who wrote one of the most interesting and compelling elephant-hunting stories ever. Ian was a poacher in his youth, and his experiences

hunting ivory in the Zambezi Valley are faithfully recorded in *Months of the Sun.* Ian's escapades while hunting elephant, without a doubt, equal those of either Walter Bell or James Sutherland. We are glad to report that the third edition of Ian's book will see the light of day in 2006.

When I turned forty, I took my family on a safari to Zimbabwe, and there we met Peter Flack, who had flown up to Harare from South Africa specifically to meet us. Peter gave us his first manuscript then, which became *Heart of an African Hunter* (volume 28 in this series). He quickly followed that success with *Tales of a Trophy Hunter in Africa* (volume 44), and we are happy to say that he is working on his third volume of African hunting stories as we write these lines. Peter never was or will be a professional hunter, but he is at the forefront of a new, emerging generation of Africans who love to hunt on their own continent and do so with a great deal of enthusiasm. It is fair to say that Peter Flack as a sport hunter has more experience hunting in Africa than any other African active in our fraternity. His books have been read all over the world, and we are very happy to have his perspective on African hunting in our series.

Hunting the Big Five by Robin Hurt is easily the most expensive and one of the most involved projects we ever published. It is our first and only title done letterpress (nineteenth century printing process, hand typeset using lead) and with hand-colored plates. There were two versions of this title, and the full-leather edition (26 copies) sold out within months after we had announced it and a year ahead of when the book actually came out in print! A publisher should always be pleased if a book sells well, but clearly we underestimated the market for the full-leather version with hand-colored plates. We could easily have sold three times the number we issued. We did a further 350 copies in three-quarter leather with copper-gravure plates, which also sold very well. Only a few copies of that version remain.

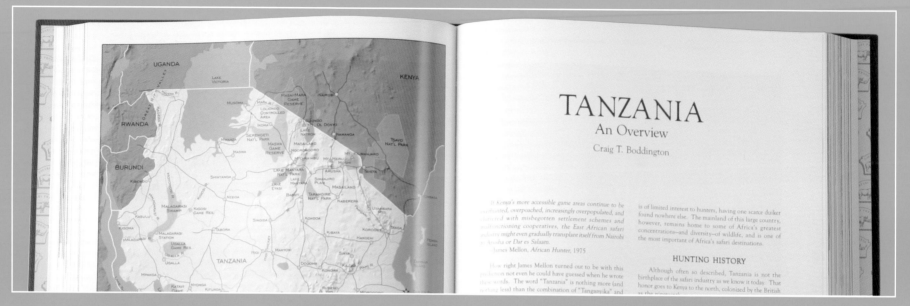

Inside the displayed book pages:

TANZANIA
An Overview
Craig T. Boddington

If Kenya's more accessible game areas continue to be overhunted, overpoached, increasingly overpopulated, and cluttered with misbegotten settlement schemes and malfunctioning cooperatives, the East African safari industry might even gradually transplant itself from Nairobi to Arusha or Dar es Salaam.
— James Mellon, *African Hunter*, 1975

How right James Mellon turned out to be with this prediction not even he could have guessed when he wrote those words. The word "Tanzania" is nothing more (and nothing less) than the combination of "Tanganyika" and...

is of limited interest to hunters, having one scarce duiker found nowhere else. The mainland of this large country, however, remains home to some of Africa's greatest concentrations—and diversity—of wildlife, and is one of the most important of Africa's safari destinations.

HUNTING HISTORY
Although often so described, Tanzania is not the birthplace of the safari industry as we know it today. That honor goes to Kenya to the north, colonized by the British at the...

Search for the Spiral Horn is a unique book in this series in that we did 1,250 copies: 250 were bound in leather and 1,000 were bound in cloth. It came with a guarantee from both the publisher and the author (Craig Boddington) that we would never reprint it. We do not know of any other company that has made such a promise. It is also the only book that covers hunting all the spiral-horn antelopes since WWII.

On Safari with Bwana Game was a particularly interesting project for me, given that I was born in the Netherlands. Author Eric Balson guided many famous people, including H.R.H. Prince Bernard of the Netherlands. Who could imagine my surprise when one day I was told that the secretary to the Royal Dutch family was on the phone! When I was patched through by an operator at Palace Soestdijk, I found myself speaking to H.R.H. Prince Bernard of the Netherlands. Luckily, I had not forgotten my Dutch! Essentially H.R.H. wanted to know when the book would be out and if we could please hurry along with it! I promised to do my best. I decided to take the opportunity to ask Prince Bernard, who had written the foreword to Eric's book, if he would be kind enough to inscribe a copy for me and one for my son, Rory. Prince Bernard gladly agreed. When Eric Balson flew to the Netherlands for the book launch, I was unable to go, so I gave Eric copies number one and two of the limited edition

of this book and asked him to ask Prince Bernard to sign them for me. Unfortunately, all sort of protocol got in the way, and the books were left at Palace Soestdijk in the Netherlands. After a long period of time, I made a careful inquiry with Prince Bernard's secretary, who told me that Prince Bernard had assumed them to be gifts and taken one for himself and had given the other to his wife Princess Juliana, the former queen. There was nothing for it but to send a new set of books, but numbers one and two are now resting in the palace library.

The last book we want to mention in this series is *African Hunter II*. Craig Boddington and I had long schemed and worked on getting an updated version of James Mellon's all-time classic into print. The project was too big for one author or editor, so in the long run we convinced Peter Flack to become a coeditor. With all the combined talent, it took us about seven years to produce *African Hunter II*—from the first outlines till the day the book came into print. James Mellon, one of the most affable and generous persons in the big-game hunting fraternity, kindly wrote the foreword. He insisted on seeing the entire book, which he scrutinized for weeks. Finally, he decided the tome a worthy successor of his original, and he wrote a glowing foreword. We launched *African Hunter II* at the 2004 SCI convention in Reno. Craig Boddington, Peter Flack, and James Mellon all flew to

Reno to help with the launch by personally signing copies of the new release. All three—Mellon, Boddington, and Flack—sat at a long table continuously signing books for hours on end . . . it was impossible to find even a short break for them to have a bite to eat. We never sold more books of one title in one day than we did during the launch of AHII. At the end of the day, we took Mellon, who had never been to an SCI convention, out to a well-deserved dinner, and he told us he had never worked longer or harder in one day in his life than that day signing books!

As we said in the beginning of this essay, Safari Press's Classics in African Hunting series now has well more than fifty volumes in it. At this point we have contracts signed for over sixty titles in this series, and we have no doubt that we shall reach the one hundred mark over time. We wish we had more room to relate interesting anecdotes on all the titles we have produced. There will be, however, short bibliographical notes on some of the titles on the pages where they are listed. Who said African hunting is finished? Certainly not the people who want to read about it!

Ludo Wurfbain, *Publisher*

White Hunter*

by J. A. Hunter

Everybody has heard of John Hunter's books because they are packed full of exciting adventures. However, very few people have ever heard of his first book, *White Hunter*. This book is a seldom-seen account of John Hunter's adventures in pre-World War II Africa. Like his other titles, this one is full of the adventures and experiences of a professional big-game hunter whose name needs no introduction. John Hunter was considered the finest professional white hunter in East Africa during his time. This title was published in London before World War II in a very limited edition, and is exceedingly rare. This is **volume one** in Safari Press's **Classics in African Hunting Series.** 1986 Long Beach, 283pp, b&w photos, 5.5x8.5, hardcover. Limited edition of 1,000 numbered and slipcased copies. .... Original Issue Price $45.00

Horned Death*

by John Burger

This is the bible on the African buffalo, by a man who shot more than one thousand of these brutes in his lifetime. Burger was employed by various companies to supply meat for the workers of the railroads before World War II, and he had probably more experience shooting African buffalo than any other person. Hunting buffalo is never easy, for when a buffalo decides he does not like you, he looks at you as though you "owe him money," and, sometimes, you pay with your life. Just as Walter Bell's name is associated with the elephant, so is John Burger's name with the buffalo. Filled with fascinating tales of crop destroyers, rogues, vindictive buffaloes, and killers of natives—Africa's horned death! This title was first published in West Virginia in 1947. This is **volume two** in Safari Press's **Classics in African Hunting Series.** 1986 Long Beach, 342pp, b&w photos, 5.5x8.5, hardcover. Limited edition of 1,000 numbered and slipcased copies. .... Original Issue Price $60.00

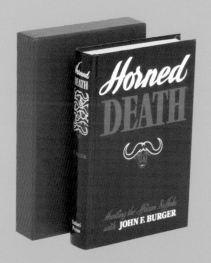

*** SOLD OUT. LISTS ORIGINAL ISSUE PRICE.

After Big Game in Central Africa*

by Edouard Foa

Edouard Foa was the premier collector for the Paris National Museum. Transversing the entire continent from west to east, he pursued his game in the area of what is today Tanzania and Zambia. Much on the elephant and other members of the Big Five, as well as plains game such as Lichtenstein hartebeest, kudu, eland, nyala, sable, waterbuck, etc. The entire book is printed on coated paper, so the text and illustrations are of very high quality. In addition the book features the large color fold-out map of the first (French) edition. This title was first published in English in 1899 (London). Introduction by Frederic Lees. This is **volume three** in Safari Press's **Classics in African Hunting Series.** 1986 Long Beach, 330pp, 29 plates, numerous text illustrations, gilt stamped elephant on the cover, 6x9, hardcover. Limited edition of 1,000 numbered and slipcased copies. .... Original Issue Price $75.00

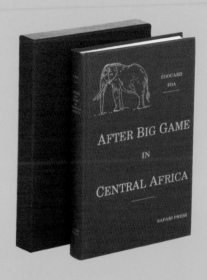

From Mt. Kenya to the Cape*

Ten Years of African Hunting

by Craig Boddington

Boddington, field editor of *Petersen's Hunting* magazine, has gathered the experiences of some fourteen African hunts in this book. Spanning a single decade, this book takes you to Kenya, South-West Africa, Zimbabwe, Zambia, South Africa, and Botswana. Boddington's personal account of these African countries, and the nineteen different available hunting areas will prove excellent reading and an invaluable reference for the reader. Topics include the Big Five, plains game, the majestic kudu, the beautiful sable, and the elusive sitatunga. This wealth of information makes not only great reading, but the appendixes also provide tips on rifles, cartridges, equipment, and how to plan a safari. John H. Batten, who wrote the foreword, said of this book, "If you have not been to Africa yet, after you read this book, you will want to plan a safari immediately!" This is **volume four** in Safari Press's **Classics in African Hunting Series.** 1987 Long Beach, Safari Press, 274pp, over 100 pictures, 6.25x9.25, hardcover. Limited edition of 500 signed, numbered, and slipcased copies. .... Original Issue Price $42.50

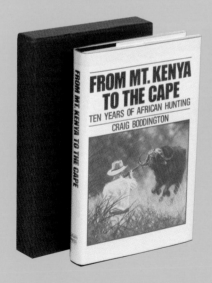

This is the only book in the Classics in African Hunting Series that issued with a dust jacket. Initially, we did not offer a slipcase, but as the series progressed we made a green paper-covered slipcase available for those who asked for one. Very few people did, and we estimate only about one to two dozen books have slipcases.

Safari Rifles*

Doubles, Magazine Rifles, and Cartridges for African Hunting

by Craig Boddington

Not since John Taylor's *African Rifles and Cartridges* has there been such a comprehensive book on guns for Africa. This is not a coffee-table picture book, but an information book of monumental proportions. What you will gain from this book is a wealth of knowledge on the safari rifle: historical and present double-rifle makers; ballistics for the large bores; what today's professional hunters use; the ideal one-, two-, and three-rifle safari setup; bullets; components; second-hand dealers; what calibers and bullets are suitable for elephant, rhino, hippo, lion, buffalo, the antelopes; and much more. In addition it contains a comprehensive survey of what professional hunters today recommend their clients bring on safari. If you ever wanted a comprehensive book on guns for Africa, this is it. Boddington is a veteran of numerous African safaris. Introduction by Robert Elman. This is **volume five** in Safari Press's **Classics in African Hunting Series.** 1990 Long Beach, 431pp, including 96pp of pictures, 6.25x9.25, leather bound. Limited edition of 500 signed, numbered, and slipcased copies. .... Original Issue Price $60.00

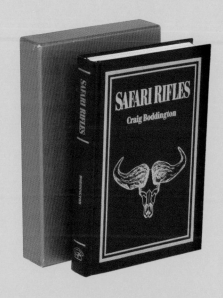

Elephant Hunting in Portuguese East Africa*

by José Pardal

José Pardal hunted for over thirty-two years in Portuguese East Africa, in today what is known as Mozambique. During the years following World War II, Pardal hunted ivory by himself with only his family and occasional friends for companions. Without the help of any professional hunter, he shot nearly 100 elephants, the great majority above-average tuskers. This book chronicles the hunting-life story of a nearly vanished breed of man: those who single-handedly hunted elephants for prolonged periods of time. Follow Ze (Pardal's nickname) as he takes the reader after rogues, lands in the middle of a stampeding elephant herd, records an encounter between a snake and an elephant, and tells the stories of those elephant hunters who got killed by their quarry. Introduction by José Antonio Martins Vitorino. This is **volume six** in Safari Press's **Classics in African Hunting Series.** 1990 Long Beach, 285pp, illustrated, 6.25x9.25, leather bound. Limited edition of 1,000 signed, slipcased, and numbered copies. .... Original Issue Price $65.00

African Country Series

edited by Tony Sanchez-Ariño

All the excitement of Africa can be found in these richly produced books through the firsthand stories of some of its greatest hunters, past and present, as selected by Tony Sanchez-Ariño. From the earliest hunters who first penetrated this mysterious continent to today's professional hunters, each gives his own account of an exciting adventure on the Dark Continent. Contributors include such well-known hunters as Samuel Baker, John Taylor, James Sutherland, David Blunt, William Finaughty, and Frederick Selous, as well as contemporary writers and hunting professionals, including Robin Hurt, Craig Boddington, Brian Marsh, Peter H. Capstick, Fred Duckworth, Harry Selby, Capt. John Brandt, Nicky Blunt, James Mellon, and Tony Sanchez-Ariño. Each hardcover volume is 8.5x11 and is lavishly illustrated by a selected naturalist artist, often from the region. Each book has elaborate gilt stamping on the cover, is slipcased, printed on acid-free paper, Smyth sewn, bound in grade-A cloth, and features a ribbon marker. The eight volumes include *Hunting in Tanzania, Hunting in Zimbabwe, Hunting in the Sudan, Hunting in Botswana, Hunting in Ethiopia, Hunting in Zambia, Hunting in South Africa,* and *Hunting in Kenya.* All volumes contain a bibliography as well as a biographical sketch on each contributor. .... Original Issue Price .. $125.00 and $135.00

Hunting in Tanzania*

edited by Tony Sanchez-Ariño

The first volume in Safari Press's African Country Series is the finest selection of hunting stories ever compiled on that great East African game country—Tanzania. An incredible lineup of authors includes: Carl Akeley, Colonel Charles Askins, Baron Bror von Blixen-Finecke, David Blunt, Craig Boddington, Henry van den Broecke, John Burger, Patrick Chalmers, James Lippitt Clark, Frederick Colburn, Arthur Crites, Gretchen Cron, Anthony Cullen, Fred Duckworth, Baron Erik von Eckhardt, Frank Hibben, Dennis Holman, John Alexander Hunter, C. J. P. Ionides, Elmer Keith, Herbert Klein, Oskar Koenig, William Leigh, Peter MacQueen, C. J. McElroy, James Mellon, Jack O'Connor, Warren Page, P. J. Pretorious, C. Lestock Reid, Pablo Bush Romero, Robert Ruark, George Rushby, Tony Sanchez-Ariño, A. R. Siedentopf, James Sutherland, Count Zsigmond Széchenyi, Sir John Christopher Willoughby, and Dean Witter. Illustrated with the original artwork of Alan James Robinson. This is **volume seven** in Safari Press's **Classics in African Hunting Series.** 1991 Long Beach, 372pp, color illustrations and line drawings, 8.5x11, hardcover. Limited edition of 1,000 signed, numbered, and slipcased copies. .... Original Issue Price $125.00

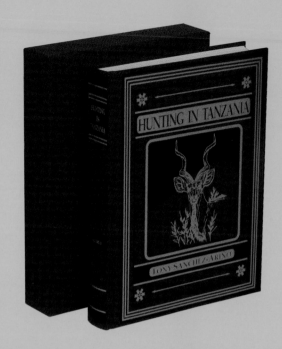

Because this volume represented the beginning of a big project, we had advance copies bound in order to approve the stamping and to proof the book. We were glad we went to this added expense. We discovered a typo on page 135: The beginning graphic in the form of a T was followed by the word "The." We had the printer reprint the entire signature of pages to correct the one mistake. In addition to the text problem, we had a problem with the foil stamping on the spine. The proof copies had gilt stamped bars at the top and bottom of the spines (whereas in the actual production run the bars are black) and the words *Hunting in Tanzania* were stamped in black with a gilt background (in the production run this was reversed). We believe four or five proof copies were sent out as review copies. We have lost track of all of them but one. It also should be noted that the initial slipcase for this book was too tight, so we remade the slipcases to fit. The original slipcases showed a gray carton face on the inside while the subsequent slipcases were white on the inside.

Hunting in Zimbabwe*

edited by Tony Sanchez-Ariño

This is the second volume in Safari Press's African Country Series. Zimbabwe is possibly Africa's most popular current safari destination and one of the few countries where the entire Big Four can be hunted. This book chronicles the earliest hunter/pioneers who were attracted to Zimbabwe for gold and ivory up to the modern safari hunter who comes for leopard, buffalo, and elephant. Authors include Capt. John Brandt, William Brown, John Burger, Frederick Burnham, John Catsis, Lord Charles Coyngham, P. H. Combe, Marcus Daly, William Finaughty, H. Hemans, Conyers Lang, William Marsden, John Millais, Thomas Morgan, Frederick Selous, Major P. M. Stewart, Robert Sutherland, Edward Tabler, John Taylor, Derek Temple, Gene Wortham, and Allan Wright. Entirely original stories for this book are by Craig Boddington, Terry Cacek, Sten Cedergren, Peter H. Capstick, Fred Duckworth, Jerry Lewis, Jack Lott, Brian Marsh, Dave Prizio, Todd Smith, Tom Turpin, and Jim Woods. Original artwork by Larry Norton. This is **volume eight** in Safari Press's **Classics in African Hunting Series.** 1992 Long Beach, 387pp, 8.5x11, hardcover. Limited edition of 1,000 signed, numbered, and slipcased copies. .... Original Issue Price $125.00

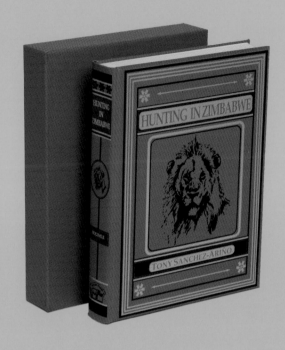

Hunting in the Sudan

edited by Tony Sanchez-Ariño

This is the third volume in Safari Press's African Country Series. The Sudan is Africa's largest country, and it contains an enormous variety of wildlife, from addax antelope in the Sahara to bongo in the rain forest. It is the only country that contains seven of the nine spiral-horned antelope as well as the entire Big Five. It is one of Tony Sanchez's favorite hunting grounds. This volume will take you hunting from the late nineteenth century until the 1980s. Authors include R. S. Audas, Walter Bell, John Boyes, Edward Buxton, Peter H. Capstick, Abel Chapman, Sir Winston Churchill, D. C. E. Comyn, Franz Coupe, Fred Duckworth, Captain Vere Henry Fergusson, Edward Fothergill, Robert Henriques, Peter Horn II, John Hunter, Robin Hurt, Robert Huskinson, C. J. P. Ionides, Terrence Irwin, Isaac Charles Johnson, Caroll L. Mann III, M. D., Michael Mason, Major H. C. Maydon, Henry Melladew, John Millais, Col. Peter Molloy, Arthur Myers, Paul Niedeck, David Ommanney, T. R. H. Owen, Lt. Col. Prescott-Westcar, Theodore Roosevelt, Frank Savile, Frederick Selous, Lt. E. M. Sinauer, Daniel Streeter, Harold Tangye, Major Court Treatt, Harold Frank Wallace, Jesús Yurén, and, of course, Tony Sanchez-Ariño. Original artwork by Joseph Vance Jr. This is **volume nine** in Safari Press's **Classics in African Hunting Series.** 1993 Long Beach, 517pp, 8.5x11, hardcover. Limited edition of 1,000 signed, numbered, and slipcased copies. .... Original Issue Price $125.00

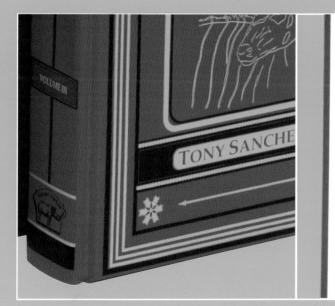

Hunting in Botswana*

edited by Tony Sanchez-Ariño

This is the fourth volume in Safari Press's African Country Series. This book contains original stories by virtually all the PHs that operate in Botswana today: Sten Cedergren, Chris Collins, Joe Coogan, Don Cowie, Willem Engelbrecht, Paul Finch-Smiles, Ronald Kays, Soren Lindstrom, Lionel Palmer, Gail Selby, Harry Selby, and many more. In addition, there are contributions by Craig Boddington, Steve Christenson, Fred Duckworth, Ken Elliott, andBrian Marsh, as well as early stories from rare and hard-to-find titles and long out-of-print volumes: Thomas St. Quinton, Arnold Wienholt, and Cronje Wilmot. This is the most comprehensive collection of stories ever assembled on Botswana! As with the previous volumes, the book contains a bibliography as well as a biographical sketch on each contributor. Original artwork by Dino Paravano. This is **volume ten** in Safari Press's **Classics in African Hunting Series.** 1994 Long Beach, 432pp, 8.5x11, hardcover. Limited edition of 1,000 signed, numbered, and slipcased copies. .... Original Issue Price $135.00

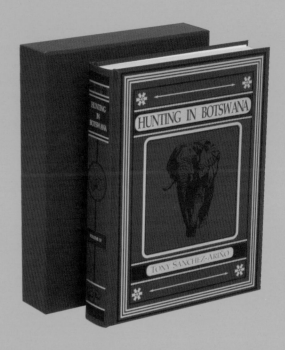

Hunting in Ethiopia

edited by Tony Sanchez-Ariño

This is the fifth volume in Safari Press's African Country Series. This is the largest assembly of Ethiopian hunting stories ever collected in one book with contributions by dozens of authors such as Major G. H. Andy Anderson, Sir Samuel Baker, James Edwin Baum, Bengt Berg, Sir John Bland-Sutton, Craig Boddington, Dermot Robert Wyndham Bourke, Earl of Mayo, Basil Bradbury, Capt. John Brandt, Alexander Bulatovish, C. W. L. Bulpett, John Burger, Peter H. Capstick, Joseph Cavallaro, Steven Christenson, Fred Duckworth, Rich Elliott, George Saint Vincent Erskine, William Fisher, William Harris, Arnold Hodson, Burchard Jessen, Bruce Keller, Alexander Lake, Sidney Jennings Legendre & Gertrude Sanford, Brooke Lubin, Thomas Mattanovich, Major Hubert Maydon, C. J. McElroy, Jack Mohr, Arthur Neumann, Joseph O'Malley, Sir Alfred Pease, Major Percy Powell-Cotton, Herbert Rittlinger, Tony Sanchez-Ariño, Rudolf Sand, Arthur Smith, Kuno Steuben, James Welch, and Capt. Montagu Wellby. Covers all the game found in Ethiopia, from the elephants in the rain forests in the east to the walia ibex of the Semien in the north. Original artwork by Joseph Vance Jr. This is **volume eleven** in Safari Press's **Classics in African Hunting Series.** 1995 Long Beach, 479pp, 8.5x11, hardcover. Limited edition of 1,000 signed, numbered, and slipcased copies............. $135.00

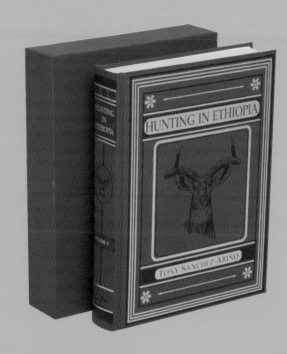

Hunting in Zambia

edited by Tony Sanchez-Ariño

This is the sixth volume in Safari Press's African Country Series, and it contains the largest assembly of Zambian hunting stories ever collected in one volume. From the death of David Livingstone to the resurgence of hunting in Zambia in the 1990s, this volume chronicles the history of hunting in Zambia. Contributors include Jack Atcheson Sr., Elizabeth Balneaves, Craig Boddington, Tom V. Bulpin, John Burger, Peter H. Capstick, Norman Carr, William Chadwick, Anne Dodgson, Fred Duckworth, Kevin Duffy, James Dunbar-Brunton, John H. Eagle, George Saint Vincent Erskine, Jeffrey T. Fester, Edouard Foà, A. St. Hill Gibbons, George L. Harrison, J. E. Hughes, Thomas Hunt, Conyers Lang, Tony Lawman, Owen Letcher, Dennis Lyell, Rory Macaulay, C. J. McElroy, James Mellon, J. T. Muirhead, Warren Page, C. Lestock Reid, Wilfrid Robertson, Tony Sanchez-Ariño, Frank Savile, Frederick Selous, William John Townsend Shorthose, Todd Smith, Major Percy Stewart, John "Pondoro" Taylor, and Lawrence Wallace. Original artwork by Elise van der Heijden. This is **volume twelve** in Safari Press's **Classics in African Hunting Series.** 1997 Long Beach, 487pp, 8.5x11, hardcover. Limited edition of 1,000 signed, numbered, and slipcased copies. $135.00

Hunting in South Africa

edited by Tony Sanchez-Ariño

This is the seventh volume in Safari Press's African Country Series and covers hunting in South Africa from 1790 to 1997. This volume contains the largest selection of hunting stories ever collected on South Africa. Contributors include Jack Atcheson Sr., William Charles Baldwin, Robert Michael Ballantyne, Robin Barkes, Craig Boddington, H. A. Bryden, Tom V. Bulpin, Joe Coogan, Roualeyn Gordon-Cumming, Diocleeciano Fernandes Das Neves, Mark de Wet, Kenneth Elliott, George Saint Vincent Erskine, Frederick Findlay, Sir James Fitzpatrick, Peter Flack, William Cornwallis Harris, Emil Holub, Allen Jones, Frederick Kirby, Paul Kruger, Alexander Lake, Henry Leveson, Capt. Thomas Lucas, Brian Marsh, Tom McIntyre, James Mellon, John Millais, George Mossop, James Nicolls & William Eglington, Walt Prothero, Tony Sanchez-Ariño, Todd Smith, Ron Spomer, Bruce Truter, Capt. Pierre van der Walt, Oliver Walker, A. C. White, and Harry Wohuter. Original artwork by Paul Bosman. This is **volume thirteen** in Safari Press's **Classics in African Hunting Series.** 1998 Long Beach, 399pp, 8.5x11, hardcover. Limited edition of 1,000 signed, numbered, and slipcased copies. $135.00

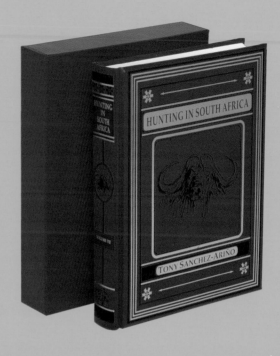

The Last of the Few*

Forty-two Years of African Safaris

by Tony Sanchez-Ariño

Tony Sanchez-Ariño has the honor of being among the elite of Africa's professional hunters; indeed, on longevity alone virtually no one has been hunting the Dark Continent longer on a continual basis. He began hunting in 1952 in West Africa, and he has hunted and guided in the Cameroon, the Sudan, Kenya, the C.A.R., Botswana, South Africa, Tanzania, Zambia, and Zimbabwe. Here is the story of his career with all the highlights that come from pursuing the unusual and dangerous animals that are native to Africa. Hunters will be pleased to know that Tony thinks that some of the best hunting in Africa is to be had today, and he substantiates this claim with his stories of guiding clients over the past few years to some very fine Zimbabwe elephants. There is much on rifles and calibers, the Big Five, and the spiral-horned antelope. Artwork by Joseph Vance Jr., and foreword by Antonio Reyes de los Reyes. This is **volume seventeen** in Safari Press's **Classics in African Hunting Series.** 1995 Long Beach, 244pp, b&w photos, 8x10.5, hardcover. Limited edition of 1,000 signed, numbered, and slipcased copies. .... Original Issue Price $85.00

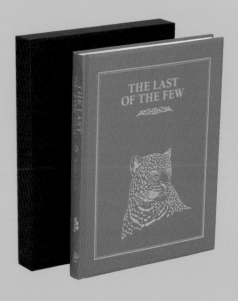

A Man Called Lion*

The Life and Times of John Howard "Pondoro" Taylor

by Peter H. Capstick

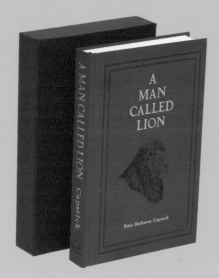

John Taylor is well known to just about anybody interested in firearms or African hunting. This is the complete biography of this very controversial character, written by Peter H. Capstick with research by Brian Marsh, a longtime Taylor acquaintance. Capstick tracks the life of this enigmatic figure from his early days in Ireland to the day he left Nyasaland in disgrace and in fear of arrest some forty years later. Also included are his wretched, depressing final years in London. Nothing is held back—whether it be his smuggling affair in Canada, ivory poaching, refusal to pay his bills, his tall tales and impressive escapes, or his homosexuality. This is Capstick at his very best on one of Africa's most intriguing characters. Artwork by Joseph Vance Jr., and foreword by Alexander Maitland. This is **volume eighteen** in Safari Press's **Classics in African Hunting Series.** 1994 Long Beach, 330pp, photos, 6.25x9.25, hardcover. Limited edition of 1,000 signed, numbered, and slipcased copies. .... Original Issue Price ... $85.00

Baron in Africa*

The Adventures of the Remarkable Werner von Alvensleben

by Brian Marsh

Werner von Alvensleben came from a long line of German aristocrats, yet far from a privileged and cushioned life, his biography reads like a Hollywood adventure movie. Imprisoned in Zimbabwe (formerly known as Rhodesia) during World War II, he escaped by digging underneath an electric fence in the rain and making his way by foot to Mozambique. He founded the famous Safarilandia hunting company that employed such renowned professional hunters as Wally Johnson and Harry Manners. Werner's safari company guided many hunting luminaries including Jack O'Connor and Robert Ruark (who found out he could not bribe Werner!). Follow his exceptional career as he hunts lion, goes after large kudu, kills a full-grown buffalo with a spear, and hunts for elephant and ivory in some of the densest brush in Africa. The adventure and the experience were what counted to this fascinating character, not the money or fame; indeed, in the end he left Mozambique with barely more than the clothes on his back. This is an adventure story on one of the most interesting characters to have come out of Africa after World War II. Foreword by Ian Player. This is **volume nineteen** in Safari Press's **Classics in African Hunting Series.** 1997 Long Beach, 290pp, b&w photos, 6x9, hardcover. Limited edition of 1,000 signed, numbered, and slipcased copies. .... Original Issue Price $60.00

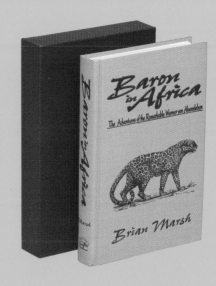

Months of the Sun*

Forty Years of Elephant Hunting in the Zambezi Valley

by Ian Nyschens

Ian Nyschens (pronounced "nations") has shot equally as many elephants as Walter Bell, and under much more difficult circumstances. His book will rank or surpass the best elephant-ivory hunting books published in the twentieth century. Remarkably, his adventures took place much later than those of the likes of Bell, Sutherland, Neumann, and others. Having shot well over 1,000 elephants under circumstances that will be unbelievable to some, Ian Nyschens and his hunts with his double rifle are sure to impress. Included in this book is his remarkable adventure when he and some friends were charged by seventeen elephants in a swamp. He was the most notorious elephant poacher in Rhodesia until the time he was finally appointed a warden to help protect the game. This is a highly entertaining story of an irascible loner whose violent adventures make Jesse James sound like a Sunday school teacher! Artwork by Larry Norton. This is **volume twenty** in Safari Press's **Classics in African Hunting Series.** 1997 Long Beach, 410pp, b&w photos, 8.5x11, hardcover. Limited edition of 1,000 signed, numbered, and slipcased copies. .... Original Issue Price $75.00

My Last Kambaku*

by Leo Kröger

Leo Kröger was born in Khabarovsk in the Russian Far East. As he says in the opening of his book, "this [being born in Siberia in 1912] condemned me to savor two great wars, a multitude of revolutions, the Soviet and Japanese occupation in Manchuria, Nazism, communism, apartheid, and the atomic bomb." He lived and hunted in Siberia, Manchuria, China, England, Germany, and, since 1953, Mozambique. This is the story of his hunting life—with emphasis on his hunting in Africa—told in wonderful anecdotes that are at times warm, personal, witty, and above all humorous. It is the story of a man with a lifelong passion for hunting and wingshooting; it is the story of the relationship between a man and his dog and between a man and his guns; and it is also the story of the assorted colorful characters, and there were many, who accompanied him on the frozen marshes of Siberia as well as in the blistering forests of Mozambique. *My Last Kambaku* reflects the richness and fullness of Leo Kröger's unusually long and eventful life, making this an engaging hunting memoir as well as a page-turner. Foreword by his friend and hunting companion for many years, Baron Werner von Alvensleben. Introduction by Erpo Freiherr von Droste zu Vischering. This is **volume twenty-one** in Safari Press's **Classics in African Hunting Series.** 1996 Long Beach, 262pp, b&w photos, 6x9, hardcover. Limited edition of 1,000 signed, numbered, and slipcased copies. .... Original Issue Price $60.00

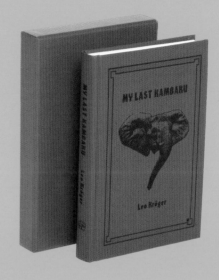

Where Lions Roar*

Ten More Years of African Hunting

by Craig Boddington

Craig Boddington's sequel to *From Mt. Kenya to the Cape* is the story of Boddington's hunts on the Dark Continent from 1986–1996. This book covers big game shot in Ethiopia, the C.A.R., Tanzania, Mozambique, Zimbabwe, South Africa, Zambia, and Botswana. From the steaming jungles of the Congo basin in search of the elusive bongo to the arid bushveld of Zimbabwe for leopard, Boddington pursues a large array of animals. America's most popular international hunter/writer tracks after such exotic animals as the mountain nyala, giant forest hog, sitatunga, giant eland, and a host of other game with unusual names. Of course, he hunts such "normal" animals as the Cape buffalo, lion, leopard, and elephant, too! If you like Boddington's magazine articles, you'll like this book. This is **volume twenty-two** in Safari Press's **Classics in African Hunting Series.** 1997 Long Beach, 349pp, b&w photos, 6x9, hardcover. Limited edition of 1,000 signed, numbered, and slipcased copies. .... Original Issue Price $60.00

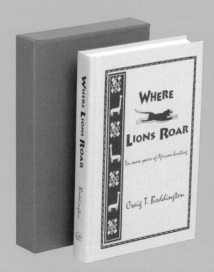

Memoirs of an African Hunter*

A Narrative of a Professional Hunter's Experiences in Africa

by Terry Irwin

Terry Irwin is no average professional hunter—that would be like saying Walter Bell shot a few elephants. In his fascinating memoirs, Irwin describes his early years as a schoolboy hunting in Botswana and Bechuanaland, his time as a prospector, and later, his employment by the Tanzania Game Department as an elephant-control officer. Although he prefers to keep his total elephant bag to himself, Irwin's feats are well known: walking thousands of miles on foot on safaris across remote parts of Tanzania, Ethiopia, and Kenya; hunting "problem" lions and leopards as well as elephants; and creating his own safari company, Kiburuzo Safaris. Irwin also includes interesting details: like the time when one of his clients took four years to bag a 100-pound elephant, and then ended up with two. Finally, Irwin shares his move to the Sudan after Tanzania closed its doors to hunting, and his subsequent creation of another successful safari company in South Africa. This book contains some of the best-ever photos and stories of large East African ivory. Introduction by Marc Pechenart. This is **volume twenty-three** in Safari Press's **Classics in African Hunting Series.** 1998 Long Beach, 409pp, 100 color and 20 b&w photos, 8.5x11, hardcover. Limited edition of 1,000 signed, numbered, and slipcased copies. .... Original Issue Price $85.00

Fourteen Years in the African Bush*

An Account of a Kenyan Game Warden

by Anthony S. Marsh

Tony Marsh is a most unusual individual. He chose a life of hardship when he decided to become a game warden in East Africa (Kenya), where he was in charge of problem animals and problem people. He and his wife came to Kenya after reading in their local English newspaper about a job offer in the Kenya Colony. Soon he discovered that the most exciting jobs were those of the elephant control officers. After acquiring a .404, he set about to learn his job, knowing that he had to learn fast or he would become a statistic. There are amazing adventures with elephants and other East African game, so follow the author as he penetrates the coastal thickets of Kenya where it is impossible to see an elephant standing a mere ten paces away. You will read about the time when he pursued a tuskless bull elephant that killed cattle, or the time one of Tony Marsh's underlings shot a 100-pound elephant accidentally while a nearby hunting client was looking for one in vain! This graphic and well-written story is testimony to a man who feels he has never quite got used to "civilization" as we know it. This is **volume twenty-four** in Safari Press's **Classics in African Hunting Series.** 1998 Long Beach, 300pp, b&w photos, 6x9, hardcover. Limited edition of 1,000 signed, numbered, and slipcased copies. .... Original Issue Price $70.00

Africa's Greatest Hunter*

The Lost Writings of Frederick C. Selous

edited by Dr. James A. Casada

For years ardent Selous fans have known that Selous wrote many articles in rare periodicals such as *The Field* as well as being a contributor to the hunting books of other authors. Now for the first time Safari Press and well-known Africana expert Dr. Jim Casada present these articles in book form. All the stories relate to the continent that held Selous in fascination for his entire life—Africa. Read about Selous's early hunting days in Botswana, about hunting the lions of the Kalahari, his many hunting trips in Zambezia, his outlook on big-game rifles, his elephant hunting adventures, his views on hippo, his presentation to the Royal Geographic Society about his hunts in Southern Africa, and much more. All of this material is annotated by Dr. Jim Casada. In addition there is a comprehensive bibliography as well as a photo section with many previously unpublished photos. This is **volume twenty-five** in Safari Press's **Classics in African Hunting Series.** 1998 Long Beach, 276pp, b&w photos, 6x9, hardcover. Limited edition of 1,000 signed, numbered, and slipcased copies. .... Original Issue Price $75.00

Buffalo, Elephant, & Bongo

Alone in the Savannas and Rain Forests of the Cameroon

by Dr. Reinald von Meurers

Many people have been on safari but few venture to take a safari alone. Dr. Reinald von Meurers's record is unique: He has been on twenty-five self-guided hunts in the Cameroon; he has hunted from Lake Chad to the border of the Congo; and he has gone after elephant, bongo, buffalo, and a host of other animals over a period of nearly two decades. Follow him as he faces bull elephant deep in the rain forest (more than twenty miles by foot to the nearest village); is threatened by a large gorilla; floats for several weeks down a remote river in search of new hunting grounds; bags forest rarities like sitatunga, giant forest hog, and bushpig; hunts for a record-book dwarf buffalo; avoids snakes and stinging honey bees; and in general has the time of his life hunting solo in one of the most remote areas left on this earth. Illustrated with dozens of pictures, this book is an antidote for those tired of reading the usual safari story. Foreword by Ernst A. Zwilling. This is **volume twenty-six** in Safari Press's **Classics in African Hunting Series.** 1999 Long Beach, 233pp, 32 pages of color and b&w photos, 6x9, hardcover. Limited edition of 1,000 signed, numbered, and slipcased copies. $65.00

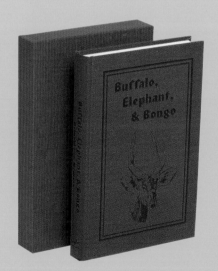

Under the African Sun
Forty-eight Years of Hunting the African Continent
by Dr. Frank C. Hibben

Dr. Frank C. Hibben was a legend in the field of hunting. This early Weatherby Award winner went on a grand total of thirty-six safaris. From his first safari in 1949 to his last in 1997, he traveled to almost every African country and hunted every major and minor game animal of the Dark Continent. From his early safaris with Andrew Holmberg in East Africa until his last hunts in Tanzania, there have been very few animals he did not take. Before Chad, Somalia, and Kenya banned hunting, he shot such unusual animals as the eastern bongo, dibatag gazelle, and addax. In addition, his collection of ivory and what is generally regarded as the biggest leopard to ever come from Kenya are truly impressive. These hunts and many more are described in his last book, which contains the best from his earlier title *Hunting In Africa* as well as seventeen previously unpublished stories of African big-game hunting and adventure. Dozens of color photos. Artwork by Paul Bosman, foreword by Albert A. Gutierrez, and introduction by James S. Underwood Jr. This is **volume twenty-seven** in Safari Press's **Classics in African Hunting Series.** 1999 Long Beach, 305pp, color and b&w photos, 7x10, hardcover. Limited edition of 1,000 signed, numbered, and slipcased copies. $85.00

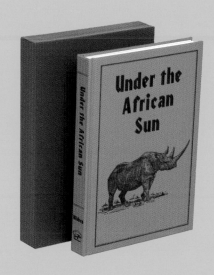

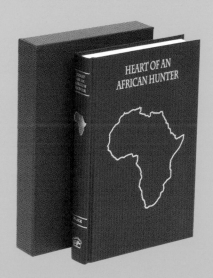

Heart of an African Hunter
Stories of the Big Five and the Tiny Ten
by Peter Flack

Peter Flack is an experienced African hunter and writer whose travels on the Dark Continent set him far above the pack. In this book he recalls his adventures in seven African countries—Mozambique, Tanzania, Ethiopia, and the C.A.R., as well as Zimbabwe, South Africa, and Botswana—where he has hunted for all game, from the tiniest and often more challenging antelope to the largest rumbling pachyderms. Besides spiral-horned antelope and the Big Five, he also hunts unusual smaller antelope that he has christened the "Tiny Ten." Although not a PH, he has shot no less than fifty-one buffalo. His vivid text gives you an excellent idea of what it is like to follow a white rhino in South Africa or a giant eland in the C.A.R. This collection of Flack's writings covers so much game that after reading this book you will agree that the Big Five are not the only worthwhile African trophies. Foreword by Brian Marsh. This is **volume twenty-eight** in Safari Press's **Classics in African Hunting Series.** 1999 Long Beach, 266pp, photos, 6x9, hardcover. Limited edition of 1,000 signed, numbered, and slipcased copies. $60.00

The Hunting Instinct

Safari Chronicles on Hunting, Game Conservation, and Management
in the Republic of South Africa and Namibia: 1990–1998

by Philip D. Rowter

The Hunting Instinct is a well-illustrated chronicle of Philip D. Rowter's hunting experiences in South Africa and Namibia, covering eight safaris from 1990 to 1998. Apart from taking the reader in search of trophy game, this captivating and highly entertaining book also provides biological information on the Big Five and most plains-game species encountered and hunted along the hot, dusty, insect-bitten, snake-ridden way. It tells the story of game and environmental conservation efforts, encounters with various dangerous creatures, and death under the African sun. The text has been forged from Rowter's experiences and is a true tale crammed full with the thrills, dangers, and disappointments of the chase. It is about the persistent instinct called hunting. This is **volume twenty-nine** in Safari Press's **Classics in African Hunting Series.** 1999 Long Beach, 237pp, b&w photos, 6x9, hardcover. Limited edition of 1,000 signed, numbered, and slipcased copies. $50.00

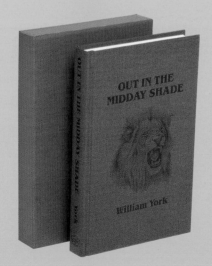

Out in the Midday Shade

Memoirs of an African Hunter 1949–1968

by William York

When he was only sixteen, William York traveled to the Sudan, seeking an adventurous life hunting exotic animals. By the time he turned eighteen, he had already shot 250 elephant. This determined youngster crisscrossed the southern Sudan on his own, with only a small band of hired help, and made a living from ivory hunting before he was even eligible to vote! Read about how he learned to feed his men after his cook was eaten by a lion; how he traversed the Lado Enclave eschewing big tuskers in favor of bulls with smaller tusks so his caravan could carry them; and why he was arrested and flogged in Uganda. After this exciting chapter in his life was finished, he went back to Great Britain for a short period. On his return to Africa he joined the Kenyan police. But the lure of the wild was still strong, so York gave up police work to become a professional hunter and mercenary. Some of the exciting adventures from that period in his life include an incident with a boomslang (tree snake) that started chewing his shoulder while he held two live cobras in his hands; in another adventure his wonderful sense of humor shows itself when he describes the time he wore a tuxedo while stalking cattle-killing lions! Robert Ruark got his inspiration to write *Uhuru* while he was in York's bongo camp. Artwork by Clive Kay, and foreword by Randall L. Eaton, Ph.D. This true-life story of a born adventurer is **volume thirty** in Safari Press's **Classics in African Hunting Series**. 2000 Long Beach, 287pp, b&w photos, 6x9, hardcover. Limited edition of 1,000 signed, numbered, and slipcased copies. $70.00

The Adventurous Life of a Vagabond Hunter*

From South America to East Africa, the Life of a Professional Hunter

by Sten Cedergren

Sten Cedergren was born in Sweden with the soul of an adventurer. After moving to Kenya, he joined White Hunters Ltd., in addition to doing elephant control work. Being a handsome devil, he had many adventures with female clients, and some of the stories you may not want your children to read! In 1977 when Kenya closed hunting, he did not part for quieter venues but rather joined the bush war in Rhodesia where he stalked (and killed) terrorists in Mozambique when he was a young 58. After Rhodesian independence, he took up hunting again. Today he is in his early eighties, and he is still hunting elephant in Zimbabwe. Foreword by David Ommanney, and introduction by Anthony Dyer. This is **volume thirty-one** in Safari Press's **Classics in African Hunting Series.** 2000 Long Beach, 326pp, photos, 6x9, hardcover. Limited edition of 1,000 signed, numbered, and slipcased copies. .... Original Issue Price ... $70.00

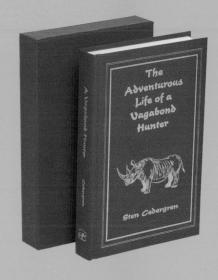

Convention scenes

Hunting the Big Five
Stories on Dangerous Animals

Text by Robin Hurt

Artwork by Alan James Robinson

Hunting The Big Five is an outstanding handmade letterpress book issued in a unique, limited edition of 26 full leather and 350 ¾-leather bound copies, never to be printed again. This extraordinary book contains the hunting narratives of world-renowned African professional hunter Robin Hurt on each of the African Big Five: elephant, lion, leopard, rhino, and buffalo. Robin Hurt is universally recognized as the preeminent professional hunter in Africa today, and his safari company has guided more sportsmen to 200-pound leopards than any other company. This stunning production contains the stories of Hurt's most famous hunts for some of the finest trophies ever to come from the continent of Africa. We guarantee they will enthrall, unnerve, and fascinate you and make you wish for more. Alan James Robinson, highly acclaimed wildlife artist, has been a designer and illustrator of letterpress books for over twenty years. The books from his award-winning press, Press of the Sea Turtle, have been eagerly sought by collectors the world over. His books are in the collections of the Library of Congress, National Library of Australia, New York Public Library, Folger Shakespeare Library, and so on. His magnificent illustrations and artwork will leave you breathless. Foreword by Herbert A. Allen. This book is a unique treasure and a finely crafted tribute to the art of the African hunt.

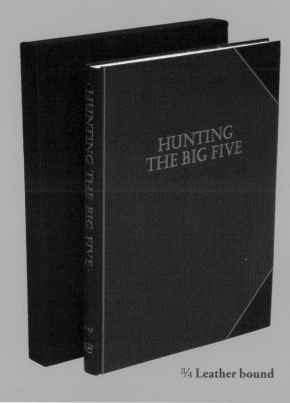

¾ Leather bound

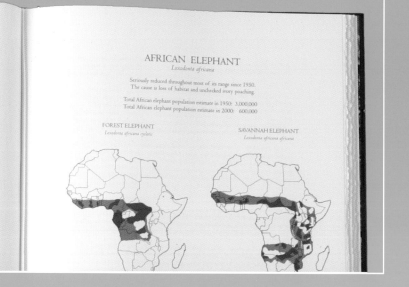

Leather bound

Specifications for *HUNTING THE BIG FIVE*

Created the way books were made one hundred years ago, this title features hand-sewn bindings, text typeset by hand and monotype, hand-printed etchings, wood engravings, and lithographs. The text, wood engravings, and linecuts were printed letterpress under the painstaking attention of master printers on 100 percent cotton rag paper, which is acid-free. The artwork bound in the book included five hand-printed copper etchings and six wood engravings depicting each member of the Big Five. Five lithographs of range maps are in full color and twelve additional pen-and-ink drawings depict scenes from the text. Every copper-plate etching by Alan James Robinson was hand printed on fine French BFK Rives paper. The book is completed by a colophon, numbered and signed by the author and artist. These limited edition letterpress books are works of art with the look and feel of a tradition long since gone. This is **volume thirty-two** in Safari Press's **Classics in African Hunting Series.** 2000 Long Beach, 137pp, etchings, wood cuts, and hand-colored plates.

Three hundred and fifty deluxe copies and ten artist's proofs were bound in ¾-leather with a map of Africa stamped in 22 karat gold on the front board and 22 karat gold lettering on the spine. The deluxe edition is housed in a slipcase. Large format in size, 11" x 14¼". $1,500.00

Twenty-six copies and four artist's proofs were bound in full leather with a map of Africa stamped in 22 karat gold on the cover and 22 karat gold lettering on the spine. Alan James Robinson hand watercolored each of the five etchings of the Big Five bound in the book. This edition contained an extra suite of detached prints, suitable for framing. The suite, housed in a linen chemise, consisted of a set of hand-watercolored etchings, all the wood engravings and lithographs, and the twelve pen-and-ink illustrations from the book. Thirty prints in all! The full leather edition and the accompanying suite of extra prints are housed in a linen clamshell box. Large format in size, 11" x 14¼". .... Original Issue Price $2,750.00*

Interesting notes: These books were extremely complicated to print and bind. Alan James Robinson did the printing of the copper-etched gravure pages. Another master printer printed the text pages with the pen-and-ink illustrations, and a bindery in another state bound the entire book, so the logistics were daunting. The entire full-leather edition sold out within months of being advertised and a full year before it was ready to ship!

The Lost Wilderness
Tales of East Africa

by Mohamed Ismail and Alice Thor Pianfetti

The Lost Wilderness is the story of Mohamed Ismail's years in Kenya and Tanzania as a game warden and professional hunter. In this book Ismail chronicles the life experiences of five native Africans, who worked with him during his years as a game warden, as well as his own experiences as a professional hunter. Read about the most deadly poachers ever seen in the history of East Africa; the best ivory trackers; the most elusive quarry, the East African greater kudu; and Ismail's dangerous hunts after buffalo and elephant. The pages are filled with the adventurous tales of brave men who always faced danger straight on—sometimes winning against considerable odds and sometimes losing, as was the case of the game warden who was killed by a poisoned arrow from a poacher. Come face-to-face with the other side of the law as you delve into the life of Tura, a notorious poacher whose limp was the result of a buffalo goring. These fascinating and engrossing true-to-life adventures of East African hunting hark back to a time that is now forever gone. Foreword by Patrick Hemingway, the son of Ernest Hemingway, and preface by Roger Tory Peterson. This is **volume thirty-three** in Safari Press's **Classics in African Hunting Series**. 2000 Long Beach, 216pp, b&w photos, 6x9, hardcover. Limited edition of 1,000 signed, numbered, and slipcased copies. $60.00

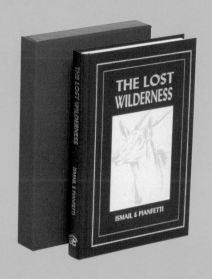

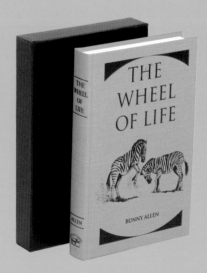

The Wheel of Life*
Bunny Allen, A Life of Safaris and Romance

by Bunny Allen

Bunny Allen arrived in Kenya in 1927 with a desire to become a professional hunter—what he became was a legend. The young, personable, and charismatic Bunny Allen with his trademark earring followed his brothers out to East Africa, and soon after arriving he had the great good fortune to meet up with Donald Ker of Ker & Downey Safaris, who gave him work as a professional hunter. In the early years he hunted with many illustrious people such as Denys Finch-Hatton and Karen Blixen. Bunny made his reputation as an elephant hunter and as an outfitter to Hollywood's stars and moguls. Bunny was the professional hunter hired for such movies as *Mogambo*, starring Ava Gardner, Clark Gable, and Grace Kelly. Bunny published two previous books, *First Wheel* (containing stories from 1927 to 1947) and *Second Wheel* (recollections of the heyday of East Africa). *The Wheel of Life* is his third complete book, and it contains some of Bunny's best stories never before published, as well as highlights from the previous two books to set the stage for his later exploits. Bunny, together with his sons Anton and David, took out some of the most glamorous hunters ever to set foot in Africa, and all the details are here—the pages of this book will sizzle under your fingertips. There are many sexually explicit stories in this book, for Bunny was the ultimate ladies' man and known for his courtly manner and luck with women. Bunny was a wonderful raconteur, and his exciting tales of an adventurous life are sure to please. This book is intended for adults only. Artwork by Harry Claassens, and foreword by Ben H. Carpenter. This is **volume thirty-four** in Safari Press's **Classics in African Hunting Series**. 2002 Long Beach, 306pp, b&w photos, 6x9, hardcover. Limited edition of 1,000 signed, numbered, and slipcased copies. .... Original Issue Price $65.00

Safari: A Dangerous Affair*

by Walt Prothero

The author, a veteran of many safaris, writes of recent real-life deadly and dangerous encounters with African critters that bite. From Namibia, Zimbabwe, Zambia, Mozambique, and Tanzania come stories that will be tagged as unbelievable by some but that actually happened—these are current tales, not stories from fifty years ago. Read about a cunning monster-size man-eating lion that finds six victims before being killed by a safari client, or about an "almost dead" buffalo that kills a PH in Tanzania who disregarded the advice of his trackers. Then there was a slightly wounded but highly agitated leopard that sliced through a slew of people in mere seconds. In another tale a safari client thinks he can kill buffalo with a small-caliber rifle because his gunsmith said so! Find out what happened. These and Prothero's own safari adventures are mixed together in an unusual, exciting, and well-written book. It shows safaris are not without danger, and you better have your life insurance paid up before you leave, because accidents will happen. Walt Prothero interviewed clients, PHs, and trackers to get the real stories, which are often more bizarre and dangerous than any fiction! Follow Prothero on adventures that will give even the most nonchalant reader sweaty palms and a prickly scalp, as well as on his more mundane expeditions—trekking through the waterless Namib, hunting buffalo by dugout in the Okavango, and making contact with Masai in such a remote area of Tanzania that they'd never even seen a motor vehicle or white man. This is **volume thirty-five** in Safari Press's **Classics in African Hunting Series**. 2000 Long Beach, 215pp, photos, 6x9, hardcover. Limited edition of 1,000 signed, numbered, and slipcased copies. .... Original Issue Price $65.00

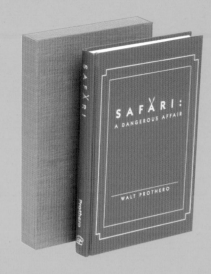

The Last of Old Africa*

Big-Game Hunting in East Africa

by Brian Nicholson

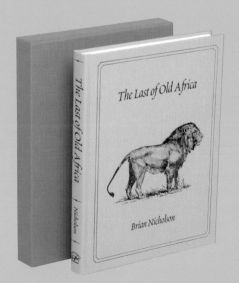

The Last of Old Africa chronicles Nicholson's career during the heyday of the East African safari. It tells of his years growing up on a farm in Kenya in pre-World War II and the exciting characters he met there as a youth: John Boyes, Allan Black, and Robert Foran of the Lado Enclave. Nicholson tells of his efforts to eradicate cunning man-killing lions and leopards, and how in the process he became the foremost expert in this macabre field. Nicholson succeeded in killing more than thirty of these menaces over a twenty-two-year period. Moreover, Nicholson did as much elephant-control shooting as any man alive today, and he has stories commensurate for a man of his vast experience. Read about the time a wounded marauder stood directly over Nicholson but, luckily, could not smell or see him. Nicholson was instrumental in the formation of the Selous Reserve, Africa's biggest wildlife area, which he patrolled entirely on foot for months at a time and eventually helped open to hunting in 1965. He recounts the biggest tuskers ever shot in the Selous, including the monster elephant shot by Alice Landreth. Foreword by Anthony Dyer. This is **volume thirty-six** in Safari Press's **Classics in African Hunting Series.** 2001 Long Beach, 324pp, photos, 8.5x11, hardcover. Limited edition of 1,000 signed, numbered, and slipcased copies. .... Original Issue Price $90.00

It was only after we had sent the first few copies of the book to our customers that we realized the four-color, folded map that went with the book had not been printed! We subsequently had the map printed, and then we sent the map to all the customers who had ordered a copy of the book.

Frederick C. Selous: A Hunting Legend
Recollections by and about the Great Hunter
edited by Dr. James A. Casada

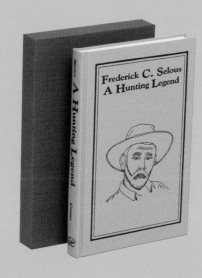

A must-purchase for all lovers of Selous! This second book on Selous, edited by Africana expert Dr. James Casada, completes the work on the lost writings by Selous begun in *Africa's Greatest Hunter*. Read Selous's descriptions of African game, from antelope to elephant, and his descriptions of hunting caribou in Newfoundland. Though Selous spent years hunting alone in Africa, he always retained his gift for friendship. In the second part of this volume, some of Selous's friends shed light on the great hunter. Included are essays by Theodore Roosevelt and the great journalist W. T. Stead, who gives a fascinating analysis of Selous's entire life. Also included is an article published in 1896 in the *Daily News* that was written by a pushy journalist who hopped into a hansom cab occupied by Selous. The revealing conversation the journalist recorded as the two rode together through London is not to be missed. The writings collected in this volume make Selous seem like flesh and blood. As in the other Selous book by Safari Press, this volume is extensively annotated by Dr. James Casada with comments and biographical notes. This is **volume thirty-seven** in Safari Press's **Classics in African Hunting Series**. 2000 Long Beach, 187pp, b&w photos, 6x9, hardcover. Limited edition of 1,000 signed, numbered, and slipcased copies. $75.00

Heat, Thirst, and Ivory
Elephant and Other Hunting Adventures in Botswana, Zimbabwe, and Angola
by Fred Everett

Fred Everett was born and grew up in the northern territories of what was then known as the Bechuanaland Protectorate, a place renowned even today for its game. His backyard was the Chobe and the Okavango Swamps, where Everett was free to roam and where he learned to hunt with an old 7x57mm Mauser. As Everett says, "So I began my career as a hunter in November 1932. Unable to adjust to the world among my own people or even a life at home, I shed the trappings of civilization like a python sloughing its skin. I moved into the bush among the animals that accepted me in my role of predator. Elephants were the only lucrative animals to hunt. As I would be poaching, I would have to be selective and take on the largest ivory, for I could not afford to draw attention to my activities by leaving too many carcasses strewn around." Frederick William Everett is known as one of the last great professional ivory hunters still alive today. In fact, Peter Capstick once said of Fred Everett, "He is truly one of the last grand characters of the African bush." Not many people can get a ringing endorsement like that! During his long hunting career, he hunted in Bechuanaland, Southern Rhodesia and the Wankie Game Reserve, Mozambique, and Sudan, shooting scores of elephants. An unusual life and a great story. Foreword by Brian Marsh, and artwork by J. Enrique Lacuesta Bone. This is **volume thirty-eight** in Safari Press's **Classics in African Hunting Series**. 2002 Long Beach, 285pp, 8.5x11, hardcover. Limited edition of 1,000 signed, numbered, and slipcased copies. $85.00

The Adventures of Shadrek

Southern Africa's Most Infamous Elephant Poacher

Ron Thomson

This is the story of a man called Shadrek, whose elephant-poaching exploits in Zimbabwe's Gonarezhou National Park are legend. In his day there was nobody to touch this poacher and hunter extraordinaire. During the 1960s and 1970s every resident in the towns, or ranches of the Zimbabwean Lowveld knew about and spoke about Shadrek. Between 1965 and 1975 Shadrek ran rings around the game rangers and police who tried to catch him. When the local black people were asked about Shadrek, they denied any knowledge of the Scarlet Pimpernel of the African bush, yet mention of his name brought enigmatic smiles to their faces. Strangely, the white community, too, despite their disapproval of his plundering of the game reserve's great elephant bulls, had a grudging admiration for Shadrek. For five and a half years during the height of Shadrek's poaching career, the author was the game warden in charge of the Gonarezhou National Park. This is the fascinating account of how Thomson tried to apprehend the elusive character known as Shadrek, and what happened to this legend of the Zimbabwe-Mozambique border. Artwork by Ilza Joubert. This is **volume thirty-nine** in Safari Press's **Classics in African Hunting Series**. 2001 Long Beach, 388pp, b&w photos, 6x9, hardcover. Limited edition of 1,000 signed, numbered, and slipcased copies. $70.00

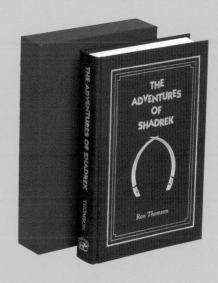

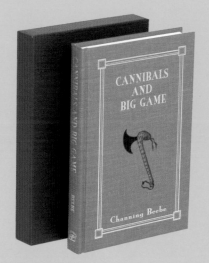

Cannibals and Big Game*

True Tales of Cannibals, Big-Game Hunting, and Exploration in Portuguese West Africa, 1917–1921

by Channing Beebe

As World War I rages around the globe, Chan Beebe and his young bride, Elizabeth, take a steamer to Angola and trek the ancient slave trails there in search of coveted petroleum to fuel the Allies' war machine. They find a brutal continent, where death, cannibalism, and deadly fevers are commonplace. Like the hypnotic beat of a tribal drum, Beebe draws readers deep into the bush, where the expedition encounters deadly denizens, both animal and human. The land is a hunter's dream, with plentiful game, angry elephants, charging lions, terrifying hippo, enraged buffalo, and crocodile-infested waters. Beebe's elephant-hunting descriptions are especially riveting, and the number of hippos he shot to feed his caravan is staggering by modern standards. With Beebe's "devil gun," the team survives a bloody gunfight with a hostile king and his savage Quissama cannibals. Lured ever deeper into cannibal country by a mysterious pounding tom-tom, they stumble upon a macabre scene: Seated upon a massive throne is a dead Quissama king, his shriveled body smoked and blackened, a massive gold royal ring resting around his neck. After Beebe and his team steal the necklace in a daring raid, they flee along a midnight trail, only to cross from one cannibal country into another. Beebe's harrowing tale and multitudinous hunts capture all that was post-World War I Africa—from the magnificent beauty of the land and its creatures to the savage native cultures that have endured for millennia. Amazingly enough, Beebe's journal with the original photographs remained unpublished for more than eighty years, but now this intrepid explorer's tale of courage and adventure is finally available! This is **volume forty** in Safari Press's **Classics in African Hunting Series**. 2001 Long Beach, 239pp, profuse b&w drawings and photos from the beginning of the twentieth century, 6x9, hardcover. Limited edition of 1,000 signed (by author's daughter), numbered, and slipcased copies. .... Original Issue Price $70.00

The Big Five
Hunting Adventures in Today's Africa

by Dr. S. Lloyd Newberry

Many books have been written about the old Africa and its fabled Big Five, but almost nothing exists in print that describes hunting the Big Five as it exists today. Well-known hunter Dr. Lloyd Newberry sets out on a long quest to pursue leopard and elephant in Zimbabwe, white rhino in South Africa, lion in Zambia, and buffalo in Botswana. You will find an interesting mix in these pages: hunting experiences of professional hunters, backgrounds on the animals, best places to go today for each species, and a discussion of where the best trophy quality may be obtained. It is laced with the personal hunting narrative of the author, who has taken numerous hunts to the mysterious Dark Continent to fulfill his own personal dream of hunting the Big Five in modern day Africa. Let Newberry tell you how you can do it for much less money than you might think possible. Artwork by Lindsay Scott. This is **volume forty-one** in Safari Press's **Classics in African Hunting** Series. 2001 Long Beach, 214pp, photos, 6x9, hardcover. Limited edition of 1,000 signed, numbered, and slipcased copies. $70.00

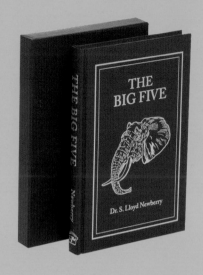

We acquire *Sports Afield* in August 2002

Search for the Spiral Horn
Hunting the Nine Spiral-Horned Antelope of Africa

by Craig Boddington

Craig Boddington is one of the few hunters who has successfully hunted each of the major varieties and most of the subspecies of the nine spiral-horned antelope of Africa. From the dry Central African savannas inhabited with Isoberlinia trees that are the favorite food of the giant eland to the dense scrublands of South Africa's Cape that are the habitat of the bushbuck, there has never been a more desirable group of antelope than the Magnificent Nine. Follow in the tracks of the dainty bushbuck, the graceful common nyala, the shy sitatunga, the marathon-walking eland, the impossible bongo, the regal greater kudu, the high-altitude mountain nyala, the princely lesser kudu, and the largest of them all, the giant eland. Boddington has hunted most of the spiral-horned antelope twice, many three times, and a few a dozen times. In the pages of this book, travel along with Boddington from the fog-shrouded highland mountains of the ancient kingdom of Ethiopia to the deep, impenetrable papyrus forest of Zambia's Bangweulu swamps. Walk alongside Boddington on a dew-covered Southern African veld on a chilly morning and immerse yourself in the most oppressive humidity and heat of the rain forests of the Congo basin. Printed entirely in color, this book was produced to the highest standards and used the best grade of coated paper. It contains nine color maps showing detailed distribution of all the spiral-horned antelope species and subspecies. Only 1,250 copies were ever issued, and it will never be printed again. Please Note: The first 250 copies were bound fully in genuine calf leather (not bonded or so-called composite leather), and the remaining copies (numbers 251–1,250) were bound in wax-impregnated cloth and have a beveled edge. Both the leather and the cloth copies were housed in a wax-impregnated presentation case. Artwork by Joeseph Vance Jr. This is **volume forty-two** in Safari Press's **Classics in African Hunting Series.** 2002 Long Beach, 357pp, color photos from the author's collection, 7x10, hardcover. Limited edition of 1,250 signed, numbered, and slipcased copies. Cloth bound.$150.00 Leather bound. $450.00

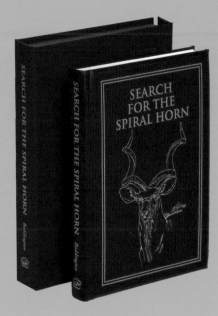

Cloth bound

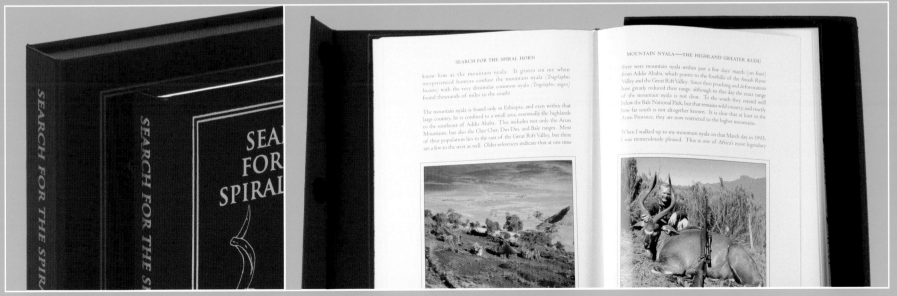

Leather bound

African Experience*
A Guide to Modern Safaris

by Craig Boddington

In this book Boddington takes us through the safari industry as it emerged after World War II, rose to its zenith in the 1960s, declined in the 1970s, and yet again resurrected itself into a full-blown renaissance to become the vibrant and vital part of game conservation that it is today. Boddington takes the reader from the glory days of Kenya to the reopening of Chad—and everything in between—covering all countries open to hunting and virtually all big-game animals. Whether the Big Five is your ultimate goal or whether your interest is duikers, pygmy antelope, or "just" buffalo and kudu, you are bound to find a wealth of information that will help you plan and focus your next safari in the right area and country. Boddington's expertise will also help you to figure out what to try for and what to leave aside, how to stretch your money into more hunting, how to plan a trip in a methodical and intelligent way, and what to do and what to avoid—he even has a chapter on safari manners! Interwoven into this indispensable reference work are fascinating anecdotes and the history of the safari industry. Lavishly illustrated with color photos throughout, *African Experience* is a book you will want to refer to again and again. This is **volume forty-three** in Safari Press's **Classics in African Hunting Series.** 2002 Long Beach, 302pp, color photos, 6x9, hardcover. Limited edition of 1,000 signed, numbered, and slipcased copies. .... Original Issue Price $85.00

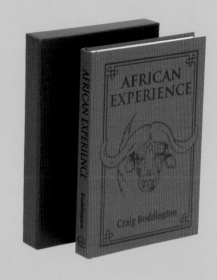

Tales of a Trophy Hunter in Africa
Hunting Stories from the African Continent—East to West and North to South

by Peter Flack

Peter Flack is a remarkable hunter. He is not a professional hunter, yet he has hunted more than many professionals. He has consistently sought the finest trophies the African continent has to offer. In most cases he has hunted species again and again till he found that one remarkable old specimen worthy to be called a fine trophy. In this book he goes after certain species in depth, such as his pursuit of the bushbuck when he hunts many of the subspecies. Then he makes a second attempt at a mountain nyala, an animal he hunts for a combined forty-two days before finding his dream bull. He then takes off on a tour for wildebeest and hartebeest—going east and west as well as south. Next is the eland, and he hunts all the varieties including the giant eland. He also visits the *Kobus* family of antelope in search of a monster waterbuck. Flack says, "every passionate hunter dreams of a 45-inch sable, a 40-inch bull gemsbok, and a 60-inch kudu," but eventually each hunter discovers that dreaming and "getting" are entirely different. The same is true for a leopard, for he again finds that there is a huge difference between desire and fulfillment. Finally he tackles the domain of the lesser kudu and the various types of African buffalo. As readers have come to expect from Peter Flack, his refreshing style brings the details of his pursuit of all these animals vividly to life. Foreword by Dr. Lucas Potgieter. This is **volume forty-four** in Safari Press's **Classics in African Hunting Series.** 2003 Long Beach, 251pp, photos, 6x9, hardcover. Limited edition of 1,000 signed, numbered, and slipcased copies. $70.00

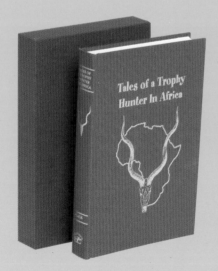

African Adventures and Misadventures

Escapades in East Africa with Mau Mau and Giant Forest Hogs

by William York

From his early days in Kenya when he and a companion trekked alone through the desert of the NFD and had to fend off marauding lions that ate his caravan ponies to encountering a Mau Mau terrorist who took potshots at his victims with a stolen elephant gun, Bill York gives an entertaining account of his life that will keep you turning the pages. York was there when the RAF bombed the rain forest to rid Kenya of the dreaded Mau Mau, and he was there to gain firsthand knowledge of some of the funny and outrageous behavior of his famous acquaintances—Eric Rundgren, Ken Dawson, Frank Broadbent, and Iodine Ionides. There are stories about how York found a cache of rhino and elephant ivory that J. A. Hunter had stashed before his death, and how John Boyes managed to exasperate British authorities with his dastardly deeds! There is an entire chapter on hunting giant forest hogs, and there are encounters and adventures with crop-raiding elephant and ghost buffalo that could be seen but not killed. As with York's previous book, the pages are loaded with interesting anecdotes, fascinating tales, and well-written prose that give insight into East Africa and its more famous characters. Artwork by Clive Kay. This is **volume forty-five** in Safari Press's **Classics in African Hunting Series**. 2003 Long Beach, 280pp, 6x9, hardcover. Limited edition of 1,000 signed, numbered, and slipcased copies. $70.00

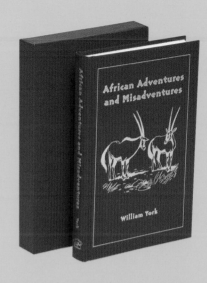

On Safari with Bwana Game

by Eric Balson

As a PH, Eric Balson guided some of the most famous people on earth on their East African safaris—Prince Bernhard of the Netherlands, Marshall Tito of Yugoslavia, and famous wildlife artist Guy Coheleach—and their hunting adventures are all told in this book. On one safari, Balson and Prince Bernhard were charged five times in four days by a leopard, buffalo, crocodile, hippo, and the same croc again! In his youth, Balson had the extraordinary job of catching poisonous snakes for a living; as an adult he dispatched man-eating lions that were thought to be under a spell of witchcraft by the evil "lion-men of Singida," and on other adventures he goes after hyena men and hunts with a Hanoverian hound named Artus. Balson devotes a special section of the book to the hundred-plus-pound elephants he hunted, some with success and others without, and he recounts the story of the biggest tusker he ever saw in the Selous Reserve—which his client refused to shoot! As a game warden, Balson was assigned to deal with problem animals and poachers alike and was at one time responsible for an area of 100,000 square miles. Artwork by Mike Ghaui, and foreword by Derek Evans. This fascinating, exciting, colorful biography of a rewarding life full of amusing anecdotes and famous people is **volume forty-six** in Safari Press's **Classics in African Hunting Series**. 2003 Long Beach, 210pp, color and b&w photos, 8.5x11, hardcover. Limited edition of 1,000 signed, numbered, and slipcased copies. $75.00

My Wanderings through Africa
The Life and Times of a Professional Hunter

by Mike Cameron (with James Cameron)

In South Africa, names like Coenraad de Buys, Karel Trichardt, Henry Heartly, Petrus Jacobs (110 lions, 750 elephants), Jan Viljoen, Major P. J. Pretorius, and, more recently, Nico van Rooyen, Bertie Guillaume, and Mike Cameron will often come up in discussions around the campfire. Mike was born in 1939 and grew up in the Koedoesrant (Kudu's Hill) area of the northern Transvaal. That was an era when hunting was a necessity, an everyday part of life, and Mike devoted himself to it with a passion. As a professional hunter, Mike Cameron spent more than thirty years hunting in various countries such as Tanzania, Angola, Botswana, South Africa, C.A.R., and Zambia. On one safari, his client and his colleague's client both wounded a leopard, and Mike was left to follow both leopards alone into the tall grass. Then there was the time a client arrived for a full dangerous-game safari . . . only problem was that the man wore a squeaky brace on one leg. There are adventures with lion, elephant, sable, crocodile, and hippo. Then there were the clandestine years when Mike spent his time fighting in the bush wars in southern Africa. Throughout his long career, the urge to see what was beyond the next mountain or valley, as well as a good sense of humor and an instinctive understanding of the indigenous mentality, saw him through many difficulties. This is a book for readers whose imagination carries them into a world where reality means starry skies, the call of a jackal and the moan of a lion, the smell of gun oil, and smoke from a cooking fire rising into the African night. This is **volume forty-seven** in Safari Press's **Classics in African Hunting Series.** 2004 Long Beach, 208pp, photos, 6x9, hardcover. Limited edition of 1,000 signed, numbered, and slipcased copies. $75.00

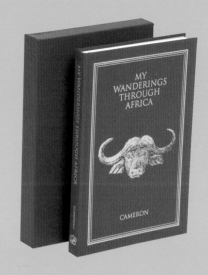

Kwaheri!
On the Spoor of Big Game in East Africa

by Robert von Reitnauer

Robert von Reitnauer was born on Christmas Day in 1933 on a farm in Mufindi, in the Tukuyu Highlands of the British Territory of Tanganyika, formerly German East Africa. His father, a German who had fought in the East African campaign of World War I, returned to East Africa from Germany in 1926 to forge a life for his family in the splendor of that isolated wilderness. But the reverberations from the drumbeats of Hitler's war were soon felt even in the remote highlands of East Africa, and Robert and his family were caught up in the maelstrom of anti-German rage. Even though his parents were fervent in their anti-Hitler beliefs, they lost everything, suffering through eight years of diaspora. What remained a constant for Robert was his love of animals and hunting, and he had for a tutor an extraordinary man and an extraordinary hunter in his father. Robert started his career by hunting ivory, not necessarily on the right side of the law, and, on his own, with a loyal crew of ruffians, he shot elephants for himself that had ivory way over the 100-pound mark. Later, switching to the right side of the law, Robert became a professional hunter, guiding clients to some immense ivory as well as what is generally regarded as the biggest and heaviest leopard to ever come from Africa. Shot by Frank Hibben in 1969, this leopard measured 8 feet, 5 inches! The book is filled with fascinating personal anecdotes: including the time a Cape buffalo lay in wait for him and knocked him about so badly that he was in the hospital for months, or the time he pursued a cagey elephant with tusks weighing 125 and 127 pounds, and the time he participated in a tribal initiation test of the Watindiga bush people by planting a chalky handprint on the rear end of a live rhino! This is the story of an immense land in the days before the truly big tuskers all but disappeared. Foreword by Michael W. Branham. This is **volume forty-eight** in Safari Press's **Classics in African Hunting Series.** 2004 Long Beach, 323pp, original artwork by the author, photos, 7x10, hardcover. Limited edition of 1,000 signed, numbered, and slipcased copies. $75.00

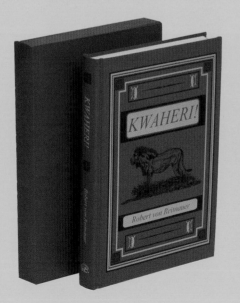

African Hunter II

edited by Craig Boddington and Peter Flack

It is with considerable pride that after seven years of work by the editors and the publisher we are able to present the new *African Hunter*. Twenty-five countries are covered, with thorough in-depth overviews of their hunting areas, background information, and best times to hunt. It includes all the Big Five (lion, leopard, buffalo, rhino, and elephant); the nine spiral-horned antelope; game indigenous to only one region; game indigenous to most regions; the rarities; the plains game, and so on—all game animals throughout the entire African continent are given close attention. There are hunting stories from each country that highlight hunting the game found in that particular area—these are thrilling stories written by people who have hunted and lived in the area for long periods of time. Moreover, you will read exciting stories of giant tuskers, huge leopards, obnoxious buffalo, a double on large maned lions, and a surprisingly nimble giant rhino. But the book goes beyond that with chapters on medical preparations, booking a safari, trophy care, the rules, and the rifles for Africa; there is even a detailed checklist of game animals, country by country. In addition there are detailed maps and numerous sidebars with immediate, at-your-fingertips information. The contributors include Gregor Woods, Tony Tomkinson, Joe Coogan, Rolf Rohwer, Piet Hougaard, Volker Grellmann, Geoff Broom, Robin Hurt, Rudolf Sand, Tony Dyer, Franz Wegnert, Mike Murray, Tony Sanchez, Rudy Lubin, Angelo Dacey, Warren Parker, Reinald von Meurers, Beth Jones, and Steve Christenson. With over 600 full-color pages, hundreds of photographs, and updated tables on animals and where they are available, this is THE book to consult for the information on Africa today, and it is sure to become the industry "standard" for years to come. Foreword by Robin Hurt with Pauline Mousley, introduction by James Mellon, and graphic design and maps by Jerry Gutierrez. This is **volume forty-nine** in Safari Press's **Classics in African Hunting Series**. 2004 Long Beach, 606pp, profuse color photos, 9x12, hardcover. First edition, limited to 500 signed, numbered, and slipcased copies. ....Original Issue Price $250.00*

Copies 1–50 are bound completely in Moroccan goat leather and have gilt stamping and marbled endpapers; they include a clamshell box lined with marbled paper. $1,500.00

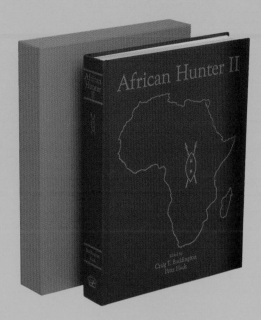

Cloth bound

Leather bound

Fragments of Africa
Vignettes from a Hunter's Life, 1939–1998
by Gordon Cundill

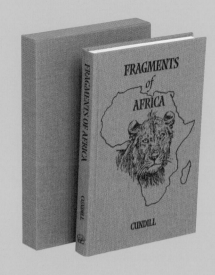

Gordon Cundill was born in Africa and learned to hunt among the Zulus; consequently, his lifetime in the African bush has yielded material for a wealth of stories. Read how Cundill with his unusual pluck and courage, faced charges by elephant, buffalo, rhino, and that underrated and yet much-more-agile-than-he-looks hippo. Cundill's interesting vignettes deal with people, historical and hunting. He includes an eerie saga of a leopardman, which almost ate an entire family; a tale of saving a maiden from a marauding python (yes, if the snake is big enough and/or you are small enough, it can kill you); an adventure of hunting crop-raiding elephants from a bicycle and delivering the ivory to the authorities with the same mode of transport; his viewpoint on dogs, aristocratic and otherwise; and his recovery from a serious wreck that nearly cost him his life. He recalls his days with the greats of the industry, such as Harry Selby, Werner von Alvensleben, Eric Rundgren, and many others. From the reopening of Mozambique to hunts in Zambia, Botswana, Tanzania, and Zimbabwe, Cundill's elegant wit paints a picture in these vignettes of African life over the past seventy years. Foreword by Fiona Claire Capstick. This is **volume fifty** in Safari Press's **Classics in African Hunting Series**. 2004 Long Beach, 262pp, photos, 6x9, hardcover. Limited edition of 1,000 signed, numbered, and slipcased copies. $75.00

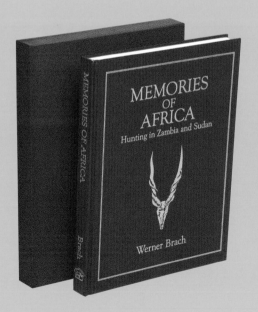

Memories of Africa
Hunting in Zambia and Sudan
by Werner Brach

After World War II, Werner Brach left a devastated Germany and sought adventure in faraway places. After wandering for a bit, he settled in Zambia and soon was pursuing a career as a professional hunter. Rather than a monologue of "I went here and did this-and-that," he gives us vignettes of some of his most exciting and noteworthy safaris. In Barotseland (Zambia) he happened on a village devastated by a pride of ten man-eating lions, and only after much work and endless tracking did he manage to kill one of the culprits! Lacking sufficient water, he and his crew on another safari almost lose their lives in pursuit of a wounded elephant. Then there was the time a client named Jack arrived and announced he wanted to shoot a big leopard, a well-maned lion, and a 100-pound elephant, which just happens to be the dream list for most hunters. A most miraculous safari followed that makes one rethink superstitions and supernatural events. A hairsbreadth escape from angry hippos while in a small inflatable boat is another of the many interesting adventures that Brach had in his decades as a PH. In all this time he operated in but two countries—Sudan and Zambia—but he knew how to get exceptional trophies. Among his most remarkable feats is the bagging of the world-record sable antelope from Zambia—over 54 inches. In addition Brach's clients shot multiple sable antelope over 50 inches. Written with an interesting flair and a true graphic perspective of the animals, people, and the hunt, this is a realistic portrayal, not Hollywood-style swaggering and gunslinging, of hunting the magnificent wildlife of Zambia and Sudan over the last three decades. Two forewords: one by Bob McCandliss and the other by James B. Barron. This is **volume fifty-one** in Safari Press's **Classics in African Hunting Series.** 2005 Long Beach, 260pp, color and b&w photos, 8.5x11, hardcover. Limited edition of 1,000 signed, numbered, and slipcased copies. $85.00

Elephant Hunters, Men of Legend

by Tony Sanchez-Ariño

Tony Sanchez is quite likely the world's most prominent, living elephant hunter, and in his latest book, he delves into the exploits and adventures of the famous elephant hunters of yesteryear: Walter Bell, John Hunter, Mickey Norton, Bill Buckley, Robert Foran, and James Sutherland. He also discusses those obscure elephant hunters who shot as many if not more tuskers but because they never wrote books are not as well known. These intrepid hunters include Aurelio Rossi, Otto Krohnert, Billy Pickering, and Theodore Lefebvre and Etienne Canonne (Frenchmen who hunted in West Africa). The late Harry Manners, also a very famous hunter himself, wrote a chapter on Tony Sanchez's elephant-hunting escapades—the last piece Manners ever wrote and something that has never before been published. Parading in and out of the pages of this interesting book are the most famous and illustrious characters to have been drawn to the mysterious Dark Continent in search of riches. Only a handful left Africa with more money than they came with, quite a few left with a lot less, and some paid the ultimate price. Being an ivory hunter was never easy, and making a living off it was a major feat in itself! However, in terms of sheer adventure and excitement, no other job on earth could ever come close to the ultimate fulfillment of hunting Africa's white gold. Illustrated with dozens of period photos, this newest book from Tony is the most interesting ever to emerge on that intrepid and now finished breed of man: *Elephant Hunters, Men of Legend.* Foreword by Ricardo Medem. This is **volume fifty-two** in Safari Press's **Classics in African Hunting Series.** 2005 Long Beach, 236pp, photos, 8.5x11, hardcover. Limited edition of 1,000 signed, numbered, and slipcased copies. $100.00

1988

1990   1992   2000   2001   2002   2005

Convention booths

Classics in Big-Game Hunting Series

The Safari Press Limited Edition Collection

Classics in Big-Game Hunting Series

After the Classics in African Hunting Series, the Classics in Big-Game Hunting Series is the second largest and the second oldest in the Safari Press publishing program. Started in 1987 with *Hunting on Three Continents by Jack O'Connor*, this series now has twenty-seven titles in it with six more under contract as we write. When we initially started the African series in 1986, we did not envision ever doing another series; however, it soon was apparent that there were many book buyers and collectors who wanted books on big-game hunting in other parts of the world besides Africa.

With this understanding, we faced a bit of a dilemma on how best to divide up the rest of the world in terms of a book series. After all, there is a lot of other hunting in Asia, Europe, and North and South America. European hunting remains of relatively small interest in North America for various reasons. Asian hunting has bloomed in the last decade with the breakup of the Soviet Union, but it too remains quite specialized and of limited interest. (We readily admit that for charm and tradition European hunting is second to none, and that for pure challenge and difficulty Asian hunting is more satisfying than any other hunting save that of North American mountain game.) We thought about starting a North American Series, but we could not see publishing enough books to make a rest-of-the-world series out of Europe and Asia and South America. Moreover, we were firm in a plan to push a Classics at High Altitudes Series, and this would siphon off some North American and Asian books. So, the Classics in Big-Game Hunting Series was born. Hunting titles from the North American continent dominate, but still twelve of the twenty-seven titles have some material on other continents, with even two books devoted entirely to hunting in South America.

It's impossible to mention anecdotes on all the books we've published, but here are some interesting notes. Easily the most dominant author in the series is Russell Annabel, one of America's most outstanding and gifted writers of the twentieth century. From 1995 to 1997 we published five volumes of his collected work. Then around 2002, with the help of longtime Rusty Annabel devotee Jeff Davis, we found another cache of Rusty Annabel material and made it into a further two volumes. All the Annabel books have sold very well, and the first five volumes are now all but sold out in the limited editions and have been selling for some pretty fantastic sums in the antiquarian market.

Fred Webb has supplied our series with two popular books on his life as a guide in the Canadian wilds *(Home from the Hill* and *Campfire Lies of a Canadian Hunting Guide)*. This descriptive writer is a colorful, salty man, and his faxes are best not read by the politically correct. The hide of a walrus would be good to have when reading some of them! His ribald comments are mostly always directed at bureaucrats, overly zealous conservationists, and other groups at the fringes of society. The editors and production people have found him a pleasure to work with, and he is always very interesting to talk to at the hunting conventions.

Sometime in the late 1990s, we received a manuscript entitled *The Collectors* from a professional hunter and tea planter who had lived in India and Nepal. The manuscript had numerous hunting stories about the Terai of Nepal, but there was a distinct antihunting slant to them. We wrote back politely to say that, despite the fact that we are based in California, we publish books only on hunting and we were, therefore, not politically correct. From this initial contact, we formed a friendship with Peter Byrne, one of

the last living PHs from Nepal. He "adjusted" his first manuscript, and we produced his *Gone Are the Days*. He now has just submitted a new manuscript that retraces Jim Corbett's famous hunts for man-eaters, explaining Corbett's actions from a professional hunter's point of view. Peter spent many years visiting all the places in Nepal and India where Corbett hunted, and he even found living eyewitnesses to Corbett's hunts. Peter is still very much involved with the wildlife of Nepal, working with various agencies to support a park and a wildlife-viewing lodge in that country.

Robert Anderson is well known in the hunting world for his sheep-hunting books and his knowledge of Jack O'Connor. It took us several years, but we finally got a biography of JOC out of him (with several chapters written by O'Connor's old friend Buck Buckner). *Jack O'Connor: The Legendary Life of America's Greatest Gunwriter* was a huge hit, and the limited edition (printed on extra-large paper) sold out within months of issue. The trade edition has been printed twice and will likely go through several more printings.

One day we learned that the IPHA (International Professional Hunters' Association) had authorized a book called *Campfires*, which contained contributing stories by many of its membership. The book was expensive to acquire from the IPHA, but we at SP felt it was for a worthwhile cause. The book is signed by no less than eight contributors, which is sure to make it a collectible item in years to come.

Very much in the same vein was *The Weatherby*, which documented the history of the famous Weatherby Award, the Oscar of the big-game hunting world. The award goes back to 1956 when Roy Weatherby of the firearms company that bears his name started it. It has grown into one of the premier events of the hunting world. The book contains a story on every Weatherby Award winner since

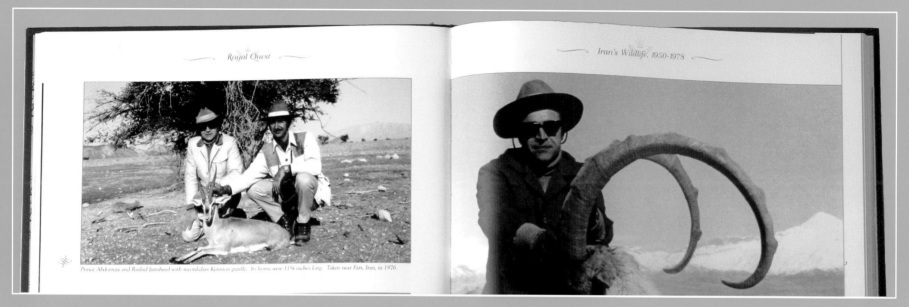

Prince Abdorreza and Rashid Jamsheed with record-class Kennion gazelle. Its horns were 11⅜ inches long. Taken near Fars, Iran, in 1976.

the beginning (except for two), and it gives a great deal of information on the number of species and continents hunted by all the winners. It took an enormous amount of research by our staff as well as Robert Anderson to gather the statistics. Again, this book was signed by sixteen Weatherby winners, which was a feat in itself!

Finally, we come to two books that were extremely interesting projects for us because of the personalities involved. In both cases Bill Quimby was instrumental in getting the books into print, and in both cases these men were internationally known hunters. The first book is called *Yoshi,* and it chronicles the hunting career of Watson Yoshimoto, a quite famous hunter from Hawaii. Yoshi had twice hired editors to help him write his book and twice the project had fallen apart. By the time we started negotiations to write his book with Bill Quimby, he had given up on the idea of ever having his memoirs in print. Bill flew to Hawaii several times to go over the enormous amount of details and material that is inevitable when somebody has hunted for close to fifty years. Luckily, Yoshi had kept good records of all his hunts. The book

appeared in print in December 2002, and we rushed copies to Yoshi, who took great pleasure in his book. We were glad we had been able to help him realize his dream.

In 1999 Prince Abdorreza's office in Paris contacted me to ask if we could suggest a person who could write a book for him. We again suggested they contact Bill Quimby, the former head of the publications department at Safari Club International. Bill and I flew to Florida several years in a row during the winter months, spending hours and hours with tape interviews as well as going over the many detailed notes Prince Abdorreza had made of his hunts. (Prince A. would spend his winters in Florida and his summers in Paris, but, mostly, he was out hunting. He hunted literally up to the very last year of his life.)

The biggest challenge was finding photos, for he had lost everything in the Iranian revolution of 1979. He told us that he had been watching television in Florida as the Iranian revolution unfolded in front of his eyes; literally overnight all his trophies and pictures were gone. Luckily, he had always sent photos of his hunting expeditions to such friends as Jack O'Connor, James Mellon, and others. We at Safari

Press thus began one of the greatest searches for photos ever undertaken. We succeeded wonderfully well in getting images from all corners of the world—Ethiopia, India, Alaska, and even a few shots from Iran that had somehow survived the wrath of the ayatollahs—but it took a herculean effort.

In the end, we published a magnificent full-leather, blind-embossed book that used the prince's crest as a header for each opening chapter. This book is truly a masterpiece of craftsmanship. Likewise, the contents of the book were exceptional, for in it the prince included stories of hunting such rarities as a Siberian tiger in North Korea, an Arabian thar in Oman, and a wali ibex in Ethiopia . . . feats that will not be equaled again, we are quite sure.

It has been our privilege to have met the people we have through the publishing of these books, and we anticipate even more great titles for this series in the coming years.

Ludo Wurfbain, *Publisher*

Hunting on Three Continents with Jack O'Connor*

by Jack O'Connor
During the years 1973 to 1977 Jack O'Connor wrote for *Petersen's Hunting* magazine. Safari Press obtained the rights to take the best material the old master wrote and make it into a book. This book contains entirely new material, never before published in book form. It contains sections on sheep and mountains, Africa and Asia, guns and ammo, North American hunting, and much more. Many O'Connor aficionados feel that his best work was produced in his later years, so this is a new masterpiece by an old master. Introduction by John H. Batten. This is **volume one** in Safari Press's **Classics in Big-Game Hunting Series.** 1987 Long Beach, 303pp, 32pp of b&w photos, 6.25x9.25, hardcover. Limited edition of 500 numbered, signed (by Bradford O'Connor, Jack O'Connor's son), and slipcased copies. ....Original Issue Price.................... $45.00

This is the only book in the Classics in Big-Game Hunting Series that we issued with a dust jacket. Initially we did not offer a slipcase for this title, but as the series progressed we made a green paper-covered slipcase available for those who asked for one. Very few people did, and we estimate only about one dozen books have slipcases.

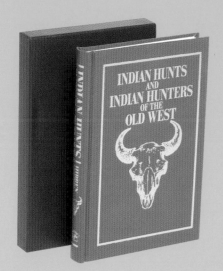

Indian Hunts and Indian Hunters of the Old West*

by Dr. Frank C. Hibben
This is Professor Hibben's fascinating account of the Old West as told to him by Juan de Dios. Juan de Dios was a Navajo by birth who was captured by the Spanish in a slaving raid. He was twenty-one years old when Lincoln freed the slaves—Indian as well as Negro. He was ninety years old when he recounted his tales to Professor Hibben as they rode to the places where the events took place. A sampling of some of the stories include: "Massacre at Medio Dia," "The Purgatoire Grizzly," "Dead Man's Stampede," "Big Medicine Lion," "Big Bucks Sleep Lightly," "The Bear That Walked like a Man," and many more. This work is a mixture of big-game hunting and Southwestern Americana. This is **volume two** in Safari Press's **Classics in Big-Game Hunting Series.** 1989 Long Beach, 229pp, b&w photos, 6.25x9.25, leather bound. Limited edition of 500 signed, numbered, and slipcased copies. ....Original Issue Price.................... $45.00

Jaguar Hunting in the Mato Grosso and Bolivia*

With Notes on Other Game

by Tony de Almeida

Not since Sacha Siemel has there been a book on jaguar hunting like this. Tony de Almeida is the most successful guide for jaguars in the history of South American hunting. He has guided some of the most famous people in the world to the world's largest jaguars. Chronicling Tony's career from its very beginning, this book will take you into the remotest parts of the "green hell"—South America's endless jungles. There you will encounter the king of the jungle, the monster jaguar, in his domain, along with other jungle-dwellers like deer, cougar, alligator, and more. Foreword by Bert Klineburger. This is **volume three** in Safari Press's **Classics in Big-Game Hunting Series.** 1990 Long Beach, 278pp, b&w photos, 6.25x9.25, leather bound. Limited edition of 500 numbered, signed, and slipcased copies. .... Original Issue Price $47.50

This book was being printed in Salt Lake City, Utah, when we received an urgent call from the author asking us to stop production. About six copies of the book were bound in green Kivar cloth *without* gilt stamping, and the rest of the bound pages stayed in storage. We gave a few copies of the bound book to the author to peruse. After all was deemed fine, we issued the order to bind the remainder of the books. Of the six original books, we have two copies that reside in the Safari Press reference library; the other four copies have been lost. All six of these books were marked "second edition," but, in fact, they were the first six to be produced . . . and that was several weeks before the leather bound edition saw the light of day.

Deer Hunting Coast to Coast*

by Craig Boddington and Bob Robb

North America's deer are the world's most populous game animals—and the most popular. But, although the deer-hunting challenge remains constant, America's deer aren't the same from coast to coast—nor are they hunted in the same ways. Join the authors as they hunt white-tailed deer in woodlots, swamps, prairies, and riverbottoms; mule deer in badlands, deserts, and high alpine basins; blacktails in oak grasslands and coastal jungles; and Coues deer in the desert mountains of Arizona and Sonora. You will, quite literally, hunt North American deer from the Atlantic to the Pacific, and from Alaska to tropical Mexico—and you'll do so with two of America's most respected outdoor writers. This is **volume four** in Safari Press's **Classics in Big-Game Hunting Series.** 1990 Long Beach, 246pp, b&w photos, 6.25x9.25, leather bound. Limited edition of 500 signed, numbered, and slipcased copies. .... Original Issue Price $45.00

Pear Flat Philosophies*

by Larry L. Weishuhn

Larry Weishuhn is a well-known writer who has hunted extensively in the American South and Southwest. In this witty, entertaining book, he describes his more lighthearted adventures, misadventures, and hilarious incidents that happened while out hunting. His reminiscences include: "How not to teach your child the ways of hunting," "Why you should always watch for snakes when hunting turkeys," and "How to use an alligator to get yourself out of a tough jam." Weishuhn's reminiscences reflect the fun and wonder of memorable days afield and the feelings and thoughts of a man who loves the outdoors and all that goes with it. This gem of a book is full of great stories! Artwork by Don Keller, and foreword by J. Wayne Fears. This is **volume five** in Safari Press's **Classics in Big-Game Hunting Series.** 1993 Long Beach, 182pp, 5.5x8.5, hardcover. Limited edition of 500 signed, numbered, and slipcased copies. .... Original Issue Price $35.00

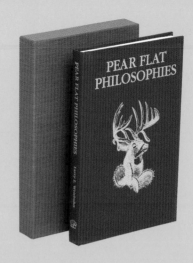

Horned Giants*

Hunting Eurasian Wild Cattle

by Capt. John H. Brandt

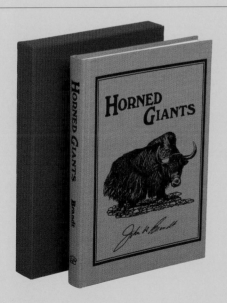

Most hunting literature dealing with wild cattle centers on the African buffalo; few, if any, books deal exclusively with the horned giants of Asia and Europe. They are equally as dangerous and difficult to hunt as the African buffalo, but the Asian gaur, banteng, and water buffalo are simply not as well known. Capt. John Brandt, who lived for years in Indochina and who is a well-known buffalo and bison expert, has brought us a new book filled with hunting stories and anecdotes on each member of the Asian and European bovines. This book also includes many never-before-published pictures of such rarities as the kouprey of Indochina, wisent, yak, gayal, tamaraw, and anoa. Captain Brandt describes the newly discovered Sao-la (or Vu Quang ox) from Vietnam, and he includes the muskox, the plains bison, and the wood bison of North America as well. Foreword by Bert Klineburger. This is **volume six** in Safari Press's **Classics in Big-Game Hunting Series.** 1996 Long Beach, 288pp, b&w photos, drawings, distribution maps, 7x10, hardcover. Limited edition of 1,000 signed, numbered, and slipcased copies. .... Original Issue Price $80.00

The Russell Annabel Series, Volumes I–V

by Russell Annabel

Russell Annabel was one of America's most outstanding and gifted outdoor writers; in fact, Ernest Hemingway said Annabel was "the finest outdoor writer" that he had ever read—an endorsement most writers can only dream about. Annabel started writing of his adventures in the Northland in the 1930s and continued writing until the late 1970s. Follow Annabel and his mentor, Tex Cobb, around Alaska as they face enraged grizzlies, trophy Dall sheep, marauding wolverines, and mad moose. No other writer has ever been able to capture the spirit of adventure and hunting in Alaska like Russell Annabel. Each volume is signed by Russell Annabel's ex-wife, Dell Annabel Lamey, and their younger son, David.

Alaskan Adventures*

Volume I–*The Early Years*

by Russell Annabel

The first volume in this series covers articles published from January 1933 to June 1951. The stories in this volume are from *Sports Afield, National Sportsman, Field & Stream, Outdoor Life, Saturday Evening Post, Hunting Yearbook,* and *True.* This collection contains some wonderful, Rustyesque titles, including "Caribou Medicine," "Wolves Look Better Dead," "Mad-Dog Hunt on Attu," and "With Moose, You Never Know." This book was an instantaneous sellout, in print less than eight months. Not surprisingly, it is now hard to find a copy, and they are much sought after. Artwork by Michael Coleman, and foreword by Duke Biscotti. This is **volume seven** in Safari Press's **Classics in Big-Game Hunting Series.** 1995 Long Beach, 351pp, 6x9, hardcover. Limited edition of 1,000 numbered, slipcased, and signed copies (signed by David Annabel and Dell Annabel Lamey). .... Original Issue Price $50.00

Adventure Is My Business*

Volume II (1951–1955)

by Russell Annabel

Most of the stories in this collection were taken from *Sports Afield,* but there were also articles taken from *True, Outdoor Life, Field & Stream, Hunting Yearbook,* and *American Rod & Gun.* Some of the stories include "Murderer in the Trees," "Trapping Is No Way to Get Rich," "Brawn, As in Bruin," "Saga of the Red One," and "Adventure Is My Business." Like volume one, this book was an instantaneous sellout. Artwork by Michael Coleman. This is **volume eight** in Safari Press's **Classics in Big-Game Hunting Series.** 1997 Long Beach, 341pp, 6x9, hardcover. Limited edition of 1,000 numbered, slipcased, and signed copies (signed by David Annabel and Dell Annabel Lamey). .... Original Issue Price $50.00

Adventure Is in My Blood*

Volume III (1957–1964)

by Russell Annabel

This is the third volume in the Annabel series. Like volume two, the stories in this collection are almost all from *Sports Afield.* There is only one story from *Hunting Yearbook.* Annabel is without a doubt the greatest Alaskan writer of hunting stories there ever was. As in previous volumes, this book is filled with plenty of hair-raising adventures with bear, moose, wolf, and sheep; it also includes his Mexican hunting tales. Some of the stories found in volume three are "Grudge Grizzly," "Death of a King Wolf," "The Curse of the Chonchos," "The Shootingest Characters," and "The Gotch-eared Bull of Toonakloot." Artwork by Louise Lopina, and foreword by Cliff Cernick. This is **volume nine** in Safari Press's **Classics in Big-Game Hunting Series.** 1997 Long Beach, 384pp, 6x9, hardcover. Limited edition of 1,000 numbered, slipcased, and signed copies (signed by David Annabel and Dell Annabel Lamey). .... Original Issue Price $55.00

The High Road to Adventure

Volume IV (1964–1970)

by Russell Annabel

All the stories in this fourth volume in the Annabel series are from *Sports Afield.* There are more Alaskan adventures as well as tales of hunting in Mexico. This volume covers Annabel's magazine stories that were published from 1964 to 1970. Some of the titles include "That Damned Diabla Dog," "The Spookiest Coon Hunt," "Black Bears Are the Damnedest Neighbors," "Death of an Injun Devil," and "Moose of the Crazy Moon." Artwork by Louise Lopina, and foreword by Christopher Batin. This is **volume ten** in Safari Press's **Classics in Big-Game Hunting Series.** 1997 Long Beach, 375pp, 6x9, hardcover. Limited edition of 1,000 numbered, slipcased, and signed copies (signed by David Annabel and Dell Annabel Lamey). $55.00

The Way We Were

Volume V—*The Final Years* (1970–1979)

by Russell Annabel

This is the fifth volume in the Russell Annabel series. Originally we thought this would be the final volume in the series, but then Dell Annabel Lamey and Jeff Davis found another cache of Annabel stories, so we were able to add two more volumes. All the tales in this volume are from *Sports Afield*, with the exception of one from *True's Hunting Yearbook.* Volume five contains more stories on the wilds of the North country he loved so much, and includes such titles as "Berserk Brownies I'll Never Forget," "You Can't Beat Luck," "Grand Stalks for Smart Billies," and "The Way We Were." Never again will Alaskan wildlife, hunting, and hunters be described in such vivid and eloquent detail, in the style that has never been equaled by any other writer. Artwork by Louise Lopina. This is **volume eleven** in Safari Press's **Classics in Big-Game Hunting Series.** 1997 Long Beach, 349pp, illustrations, 6x9, hardcover. Limited edition of 1,000 numbered, slipcased, and signed copies (signed by David Annabel and Dell Annabel Lamey). $55.00

Bear Attacks*

Classic Tales of Dangerous North American Bears

by Kathy Etling

From the early days of the Native American to modern man, humans have sought to understand the great beast of the wild, and for many just the thought of a bear attack sends shivers up even the most courageous of spines. In this two-volume set Kathy Etling chronicles the dangerous threesome of North American bears—black, grizzly, and polar—in early myths and historical hunts by people like Lewis and Clark and Teddy Roosevelt. She cites examples of bad bear behavior in literature, and she retells chilling tales of savage bear encounters that will leave you breathless with suspense. Whether you're enthralled by tales of bristly bears or just want to pick up the latest safety tips on bear-free camping, Etling's informative primer on America's ferocious bears will put you in the know. This set is **volume twelve** in Safari Press's **Classics in Big-Game Hunting Series.** 1997 Long Beach, 2 vols., 227pp & 313pp, 6x9, hardcover. Limited edition of 1,000 signed, numbered, and slipcased copies. .... Original Issue Price $75.00

Home from the Hill*

The Story of a Big-Game Guide in the Canadian Arctic

by Fred Webb

Fred Webb has been one of the best-known guides of the Canadian Arctic for over twenty years. He has guided mainly for grizzly, black bear, caribou, and moose. Fred has guided famous hunters such as Gene Hill and Craig Boddington as well as average citizens who saved long and hard to go on a dream hunt. Well known as a master storyteller, Fred has taken the most interesting, funny, and remarkable stories of his long and illustrious career and placed them in this volume. For years his articles have appeared in magazines and have won him critical acclaim, and this book contains some of the best Fred Webb stories that have made him a favorite guide and writer all over North America. We consider this book a marvelous piece of storytelling. Artwork by Tom Hennessey, foreword by Jim Rikhoff, and editor's note by Craig Boddington. This is **volume thirteen** in Safari Press's **Classics in Big-Game Hunting Series.** 1997 Long Beach, 283pp, b&w photos, illustrations, 6x9, hardcover. Limited edition of 1,000 signed, numbered, and slipcased copies............................... Original Issue Price $50.00

American Man-Killers

True Stories of a Dangerous Wilderness

by Don Zaidle

Most people think of nature and wilderness as a place where animals and humans can play and peacefully coexist. Yet at the end of the twentieth century, it turns out animals and people do not live in peace as often as the television shows would have us believe. Dozens of times each year people are attacked and not infrequently killed by cougars, bears, and sundry other aggressive critters (dogs, birds, crocs, alligators, and even deer). Don Zaidle has done a masterful job of describing and analyzing what happened and why. His prose is hair-raising in its suspense and candor. All stories in his book are based on actual encounters, which makes the book all the more chilling and worthwhile. After reading this, you will take a whole new look at Mother Nature, and you may never look at any wild animal in the same way again! Foreword by Craig Boddington. This is **volume fourteen** in Safari Press's **Classics in Big-Game Hunting Series.** 1997 Long Beach, 240pp, illustrations, 6x9, hardcover. Limited edition of 500 signed, numbered, and slipcased copies.. $60.00

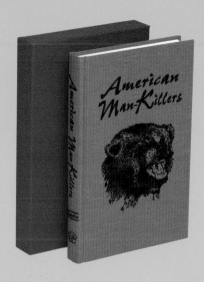

Some Bears Kill

True Life Tales of Terror

by Larry Kaniut

Never before have so many exciting, hair-raising tales of bear encounters been collected in one book. Read about a man who swam into a lake to try to escape a furious bear only to find to his horror that bears can swim too. Or of the old gold prospector who got mauled and sewed up his own stomach—and lived to tell about it! When a bear attacks, it does so with devastating ferocity. Although the average attack lasts but thirty seconds, grievous injury can result from powerful paws and jaws. Strangely enough, most attacks are nonfatal. This book is filled with true-life episodes of close calls, maulings, and deaths by all three North American bears: black, grizzly, and polar. These stories are not fiction. All are, eerily enough, based on complete fact. Even the FOX TV show *When Animals Attack* uses Kaniut's material for their shows. Kaniut is the author of two previous bestselling books on dangerous bears. Foreword by Wayne Anthony Ross. This is **volume fifteen** in Safari Press's **Classics in Big-Game Hunting Series.** 1997 Long Beach, 313pp, b&w photos, 6x9, hardcover. Limited edition of 500 signed, numbered, and slipcased copies... $60.00

The Jungle Hunter

Big-Game Hunting in South America

by Joe Cavanaugh

Joe Cavanaugh has wandered around and lived in Central and South America in pursuit of adventure and unusual game for more than a decade. He has visited and hunted (often with native hunters) in every major South American country from Belize to Columbia and the Amazon Basin to Bolivia. Cavanaugh has hunted all the native game of South America as well as the introduced water buffalo. Whatever he hunted, the excitement of the chase and the jungle were foremost. Armed with only a shotgun, he has pursued giant tapirs at remote salt licks with native hunters; he has followed jaguar and puma in a canoe and on foot aided by dogs (no book on South America is complete without a good deal on these two large cats); and he has tracked deep into the jungle after tropical white-tailed deer, marsh deer, the shy and elusive brocket, and peccary. His many trips and hunts have allowed him to make observations on all the game of the vast and unexplored continent, including those no longer hunted, such as the spectacled bear, huemul, and pudu. There are some great photographs of animals, natives, and jungles taken against a background of some of the wildest regions left on earth. This is a thorough and complete work on all the large game animals native to South America. This is **volume sixteen** in Safari Press's **Classics in Big-Game Hunting Series.** 2000 Long Beach, 406pp, profuse photos, 6x9, hardcover. Limited edition of 1,000 signed, numbered, and slipcased copies. $70.00

Campfire Lies of a Canadian Hunting Guide*

Forty Years in the Life of a Guide in the North Country

by Fred Webb

This is the sequel to *Home from the Hill.* Fred Webb once commented on his marriage by saying, "Irene and I had the typical teenage marriage that wasn't supposed to last six months. I guess the secret is that out of the past forty years I have been away about thirty-five of them." And away from home he has been, first as a radio operator in the remote North, then as a lumberjack, and later yet as a sailor. Eventually he became a full-time guide traveling all over the Arctic, guiding for the great game of the North—caribou, moose, polar bear, muskox, and grizzly. In these pages you will find the same irresistible attraction as you did in Fred's earlier book, *Home from the Hill.* In his sequel, Fred will again royally entertain you with his wild hunting tales and his adventurous vagabond existence. Fred, a master writer whose stories have been praised time and time again in the press, rates as one of the best sporting writers alive today. Artwork by Tom Hennessey, foreword by Tom Hennessey, and preface by Harry Tennison. This is **volume seventeen** in Safari Press's **Classics in Big-Game Hunting Series.** 2000 Long Beach, 311pp, b&w photos, 6x9, hardcover. Limited edition of 1,000 signed, numbered, and slipcased copies. .... Original Issue Price $50.00

Gone Are the Days

Jungle Hunting for Tiger and Other Game in India and Nepal, 1948–1969

by Peter Byrne

Peter Byrne has led the life most of us can only dream about. After World War II he returned to Ireland, but being restless, he decided to find a job that would take him to exotic lands. Using his family's connections, he was hired as a manager on a huge Indian tea plantation in the Himalayan foothills—a posh job that came with seventeen servants and a mansion. Almost immediately on arrival he was plunged into Indian jungle hunting, his primary love, when the local villagers turned to him with a plea to eliminate a rogue boar. Read his exciting description of how he jumped from a tree and sliced the boar's skull in two while half the adult males of the village stayed in the trees to watch and cheer him on. Share his many adventures in India with tiger, elephant, and leopard, and see how a fortuitous championing of a member of the ruling elite of Nepal during a bar brawl prompted Peter to move to Nepal and become a professional hunter there. Move with him to Nepal where he was, for years, the only authorized professional hunter to operate in that country. In the unspoiled wilderness of the White Grass Plains area of Nepal, where there were virtually no roads and the natives did not even know the name of the capital of the country, he hunted tiger right up till the close of tiger hunting in 1969. Follow his exploits in the Terai (forested southlands of Nepal) where he encountered a man-eater . . . that was eventually killed by a train! This is the true-life story about a time that now is completely gone—a time when virtually no cars were seen in the remote areas of India and Nepal, a time when tiger, gaur, leopard, sambar, and many other jungle denizens were plentiful beyond description. Those days are truly gone. Foreword by Charlton Heston. This is **volume eighteen** in Safari Press's **Classics in Big-Game Hunting Series.** 2001 Long Beach, 342pp, b&w photos and illustrations, 6x9, hardcover. Limited edition of 1,000 signed, numbered, and slipcased copies. $70.00

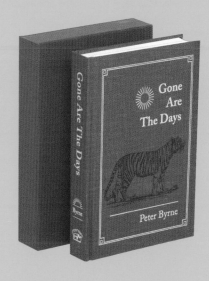

Hunting the Alaskan High Arctic*

Big-Game Hunting for Grizzly, Dall Sheep, Moose, Caribou, and Polar Bear in the Arctic Circle

by Scott Haugen

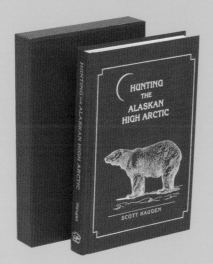

He has faced man-eating lions in Africa and has hunted in the world's most challenging terrain, but Haugen came closest to death in an Arctic storm. Alaska—a hunter's paradise set in an unforgiving climate—required Haugen to sharpen his prowess as he pursued polar bear, caribou, grizzly, wolverine, moose, Fannin and Dall sheep, tundra wolf, and white fox. Stationed as teachers in the remotest parts of Alaska, Haugen and his wife spent three years in Point Lay and four years among the Inupiat Eskimos in the remote village of Anaktuvuk Pass, teaching the children of one of the world's last true hunting cultures. Invited to hunt with the Eskimos of the Alaskan Arctic, he encountered caribou, bear, and sheep that had never before set eyes on a human, so remote were the areas he frequented. This book is for those who would scale near-vertical cliffs after Dall ram . . . hunt in whiteout conditions as windchill dips off the charts . . . race against time to stalk and field dress in agonizing cold . . . and risk life and limb for the thrill of the hunt. Foreword by Craig Boddington. This is **volume nineteen** in Safari Press's **Classics in Big-Game Hunting Series.** 2000 Long Beach, 240pp, b&w photos, 6x9, hardcover. Limited edition of 1,000 signed, numbered, and slipcased copies. .... Original Issue Price ... $65.00

Hunting the Land of the Midnight Sun

A Collection of Hunting Adventures from the Alaska Professional Hunters' Association

by the Alaska Professional Hunters' Association

This unique book contains thirty-seven stories from dozens of members of the famous Alaska Professional Hunters' Association. Specifically written to raise funds for the APHA, it contains some of the funniest, scariest, most dramatic, and most vainglorious big-game hunting stories ever to come from Alaska. Caribou and moose traipse in front of the reader's eyes, while bears and wolves parade in and out of the narratives. Through it all, the wild, savage beauty of the land of the midnight sun and the last great wilderness left on earth comes sharply into focus as each hunter pursues his quarry. Contains contributions by Rob Holt, Gary King, Gary LaRose, Garth Larsen, Jim Shockey, Jeff Davis, and many others. All royalties go to the APHA. Artwork by T. Marcotte. This is **volume twenty** in Safari Press's **Classics in Big-Game Hunting Series.** 2002 Long Beach, 293pp, b&w photos, 6x9, hardcover. Limited edition of 1,000 signed, numbered, and slipcased copies. $65.00

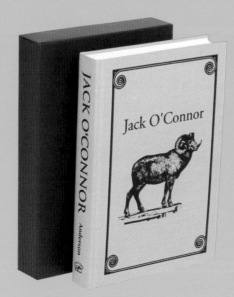

Jack O'Connor*

The Legendary Life of America's Greatest Gunwriter

by Robert Anderson

Jack O'Connor was the preeminent North American big-game hunter and gunwriter of the twentieth century, and this biography is filled with fascinating facts and stories about this controversial character. Find out how many (desert) sheep and Grand Slams O'Connor really killed; how he shot the same sable antelope twice (ten years apart!); how his absentmindedness led him to lose his car; and how he shot his own toe off. There were the glory years after World War II as O'Connor undeniably rose to the top of his profession, when he and Eleanor hunted tiger in India, sheep in Iran, buffalo in Tanganyika, and became acquainted with princes and potentates as well as the moguls of the hunting and firearms industries. His stories in *Outdoor Life* could make or break a product and moved thousands of readers to book a hunt or buy a gun. Illustrated with dozens of never-before-seen photos made available by the family, Jack O'Connor's biography includes an extensive timeline that lists the major game animals he shot, the guns he owned, the trips he took, and the books he wrote. Foreword by Angus Cameron, and special contributions by Eldon "Buck" Buckner. This is **volume twenty-one** in Safari Press's **Classics in Big-Game Hunting Series.** 2002 Long Beach, 264pp & 96pp of photos, 7x10, hardcover. Limited edition of 1,000 signed, numbered, and slipcased copies. .... Original Issue Price $85.00

Return to Toonaklut*

The Russell Annabel Story

by Jeff Davis

Russell Annabel is by any account one of the most colorful and controversial characters ever to set foot in Alaska. Rusty moved to Alaska as a teen and soon started writing stories about hunting in the Northland, mainly for *Sports Afield.* These were among the best-written outdoor stories of the twentieth century, and they made his reputation far and wide. From his homestead in Toonaklut, he could describe a wilderness populated with majestic Dall sheep, ornery moose, dumbbell caribou, and enraged grizzlies as no other man could. Based on interviews with Rusty's American wife and his recently discovered Mexican family, and illustrated with rare photos, this is the story of the man behind the legend, and it is as fascinating as any tale Rusty Annabel ever spun for the sporting magazines. This book is illustrated with dozens of never-before-published original photos of Rusty, Tex Cobb, and the Alaska they loved. Artwork by Louise Lopina. This is **volume twenty-two** in Safari Press's **Classics in Big-Game Hunting Series.** 2002 Long Beach, 324pp, photos, 6x9, hardcover. Limited edition of 500 signed, numbered, and slipcased copies. ...._{Original Issue Price}...... $60.00

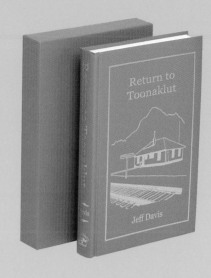

Campfires

The Book of the International Professional Hunters' Association (IPHA)

edited by Brooke ChilversLubin

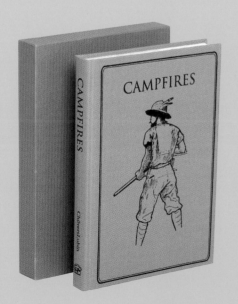

The IPHA was formed in 1969 to promote ethical hunting, and since that time the IPHA has become the most respected of all professional hunting organizations. This remarkable collection contains the most interesting stories from the membership of the past thirty years. Giant brown bears in the frozen North, huge argali sheep from the depths of Central Asia, man-eating lions from Central Africa, swamp-dwelling elephants from Botswana, snow-white Dall sheep near the Arctic Circle, buffalo in the African veld, polar bear on the permanently frozen ice, and so on. Contributors include Terry Pierson, Tony Sanchez-Ariño, Adelino Pires, Sergio Almeida, Rudy Lubin, Peter Johnstone, Mark Kyriacou, Fred Webb, Joe Klutsch, Jerome Knap, John Brandt, John Kingsley-Heath, Don Grobler, Joe Coogan, Craig Boddington, Coenraad Vermaak, Brooke ChilversLubin, Jack Atcheson Jr., and many others. This limited edition is signed by no less than eight contributing members of the IPHA. Artwork by Guy Coheleach, preface by Basie Maartens, and introduction by Eduardo Fernandez de Araoz y Diez de Rivera. This is **volume twenty-three** in Safari Press's **Classics in Big-Game Hunting Series.** 2003 Long Beach, 306pp, photos, 7x10, hardcover. Limited edition of 1,000 signed, numbered, and slipcased copies. $100.00

Yoshi

The Life and Travels of an International Trophy Hunter

by Watson Yoshimoto (with Bill Quimby)

Watson T. Yoshimoto, a native Hawaiian, collected all sixteen major varieties of the world's wild sheep and most of the many types of goat, ibex, bear, antelope, and antlered game of Asia, Europe, North America, South America, and the South Pacific . . . as well as the African Big Five. Follow Yoshi as he finds himself cut off from safety when the ice separates while he is hunting polar bears off the Russian coast. Experience his hunts for bharal at 18,000 feet in the Himalayas; tigers, gaurs, and wild Asian buffalo in India; an elephant with ivory weighing 127 and 123 pounds in Tanzania; and a near-world-record giant eland from the C.A.R. When Yoshi ended a half century of hunting in 1995 at age 86, he had taken nearly 200 species of big game in forty-three countries on six continents. This is an interesting and highly readable book about the life of one of the best-known trophy hunters of the twentieth century. Foreword by Bert Klineburger. This is **volume twenty-four** in Safari Press's **Classics in Big-Game Hunting Series.** 2003 Long Beach, 298pp, color and b&w photos, 7x10, hardcover. Limited edition of 1,000 signed, numbered, and slipcased copies... $85.00

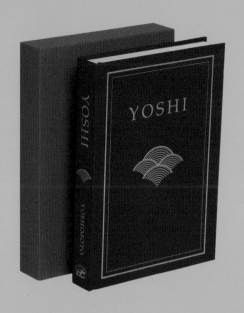

Business and marketing offices at Safari Press 1985–2005

Royal Quest

The Hunting Saga of H.I.H. Prince Abdorreza of Iran

by Bill Quimby

His Imperial Highness, Prince Abdorreza of Iran was an internationally known big-game hunter famous for his startling world records and the diverse nature of his hunts. Prince Abdorreza was the first hunter after World War II to hunt Marco Polo sheep in Afghanistan and the Russian Pamirs. He was privileged to hunt some of the most unusual animals on earth for the National Museum of Iran: Arabian thar; Siberian tiger; all subspecies of markhor; just about every sheep in Asia, and all the sheep of Africa, Europe, and North America. His list of accomplishments is long, including no less than four expeditions to the Pamirs after Marco Polo sheep; pioneering hunts in the Tian Shan of China and Siberia as early as the 1970s; all the spiral-horned antelope of Africa; no less than twelve tigers; the walia or Ethiopian ibex; banteng in Indonesia; and gaur in Nepal. The prince hunted with the greats of the big-game hunting world such as Syd Downey, Pinnell & Talifson, Jack O'Connor, Elgin Gates, and Herb Klein. James Mellon accompanied the prince on several expeditions, and some of the hunts these two men experienced in Oman, Pakistan, and Peru will never be repeated. The prince hunted wild yak and chiru antelope in Tibet, shot a 65-plus-inch kudu, and made several trips for a 50-inch buffalo. This book, written by the former editor of *Safari* magazine, is based upon countless hours of taped interviews and complete access to Prince Abdorreza's photo albums and diaries. Two forewords: one by H.I.H. Prince Abdorreza and one by James Mellon. This is **volume twenty-five** in Safari Press's **Classics in Big-Game Hunting Series.** 2004 Long Beach, 324pp, profuse color and b&w photos, 10x11, hardcover. Limited edition of 500 signed (by Prince Abdorreza and Bill Quimby), numbered, and slipcased or boxed copies. Copies 1–50 are bound completely in Moroccan goat leather with gilt stamping and marbled endpapers; they include a clamshell box lined with marbled paper. $1,250.00
Copies 51–500 are cloth bound with gilt stamping and a slipcase. $325.00

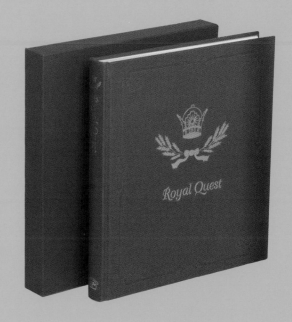

Cloth bound

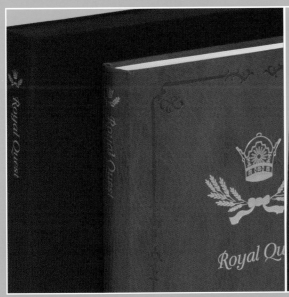

Leather bound

To Heck with It, I'm Going Hunting

My First Eighteen Years as an International Big-Game Hunter

by Arnold Alward (with Bill Quimby)

Arnold Alward has taken nearly all the world's important big-game species, eventually winning the Weatherby Award. During the course of his hunts, he shot a Grand Slam and a Super Slam of Sheep, the Big Five, as well as all the spiral-horned antelope of Africa. His busiest year was 1988, when he made thirteen major hunts! When he went on safari to Ethiopia, he passed up a 75-pound elephant before taking a 110 x 115-pound tusker on the tenth day of the hunt; then he continued in that country to take a mountain nyala. After Ethiopia, he successfully hunted caribou in the Northwest Territories, the Yukon, and Quebec; a whitetail in Alberta; Columbia blacktails and brown bears on Alaska's Kodiak Island; and Coues deer in Mexico . . . all in the same year! In Asia, he hunted most of the major sheep species that inhabit the High Altai, the Pamirs, and the Tibetan Plateau. During one of his trips to Mongolia, he took Altai and Gobi argali, Siberian roe deer, and maral stag. Alward's hunts were always full of adventure: He landed in Zambia during a rebellion, when dissenters seized a TV station and the government rolled tanks out in the streets, and just before he reached his hunting camp on that trip local wardens killed several poachers. He also hunted in Sudan during one of its civil wars . . . all in all, he's had an adventurous time. Foreword by Chuck Bazzy. This is **volume twenty-six** in Safari Press's **Big-Game Hunting Series.** 2003 Long Beach, 316pp, profuse color and b&w photos, 7x10, hardcover. Limited edition of 1,000 signed, numbered, and slipcased copies.. $80.00

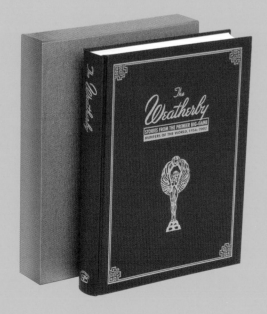

The Weatherby

Stories from the Premier Big-Game Hunters of the World, 1956–2002

edited by Nancy Vokins

For nearly fifty years, the Weatherby Award has been known as the Oscar of the hunting world in recognition of the achievements of the world's greatest hunters. From Herb Klein's first award in 1956 to Rex Baker's award in 2002, all the award winners are included. There are stories on how James Mellon (1972) pursued a giant markhor in Afghanistan with dogged determination; how Carlo Caldesi (1981) shot a gaur that got singed in a brush fire; how Prince Abdorreza (1962) searched for a world-record Persian ibex; how Frank Hibben (1964) stalked an immense tiger, but ended up with the largest leopard ever taken in his time; how Thornton Snider (1985) found an elephant with monster tusks; how Rudolf Sand (1976) pursued an impossible-to-get mountain nyala; and what happened on C. J. McElroy's (1969), founder of SCI, last safari in Africa. A grand total of forty-six interesting stories and biographies, a historical introduction as to how the Weatherby originated, hundreds of fascinating photographs, and statistical information and background on the award are included. This limited edition has been signed by no less than sixteen Weatherby winners, a unique feat in book publishing and sure to make this book a superb collector's item in years to come. Foreword by Andy Oldfield, and introduction by Robert Anderson. This is **volume twenty-seven** in Safari Press's **Classics in Big-Game Hunting Series.** 2004 Long Beach, 434pp, color and b&w photos, 8.5x11, hardcover. Limited edition of 1,000 signed, numbered, and slipcased copies. $200.00

Craig Boddington & his daughter Brittany

Bill York

Tony Sanchez-Ariño

Peter Capstick

Robert Anderson

Kevin Robertson

Robin Hurt & his wife, Pauline

H.I.H. Prince Abdorreza

J. Y. Jones

Sten Cedergren & Walt Prothero

H.I.H. Prince Abdorreza & Bill Quimby

Gordon Cundill

Peter Flack & James Mellon

Scott Haugen

Jesús Yurén & his wife, Pita

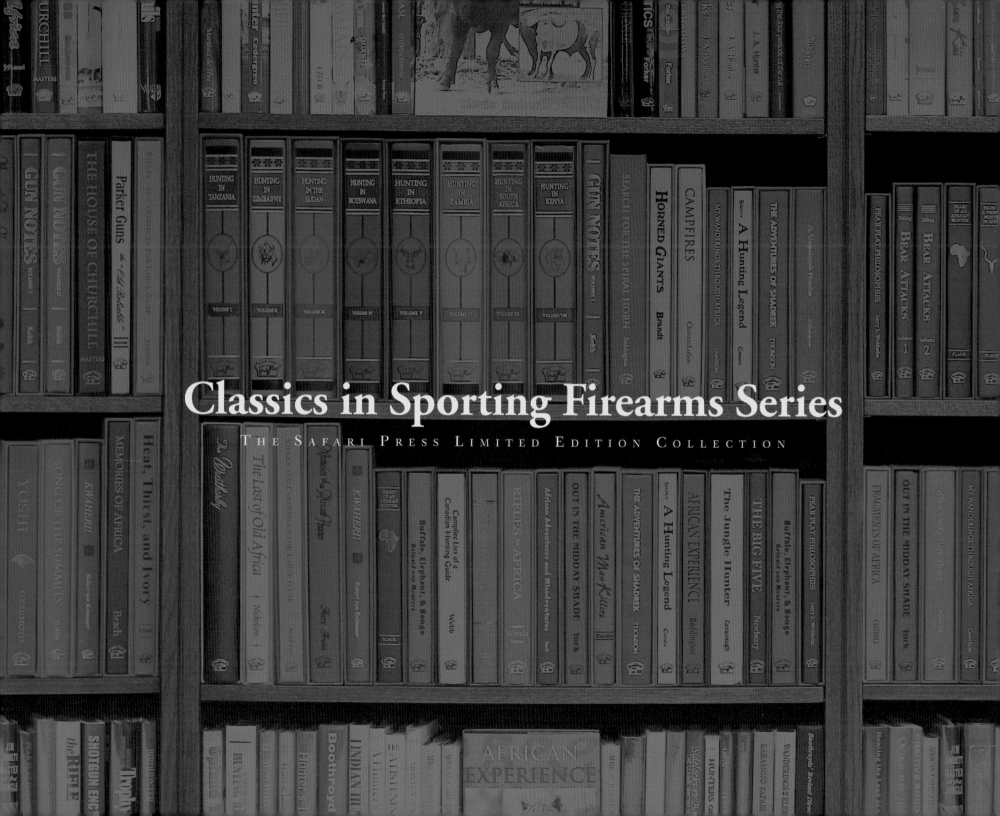

Classics in Sporting Firearms Series

THE SAFARI PRESS LIMITED EDITION COLLECTION

Classics in Sporting Firearms, Hunting at High Altitudes, and Wingshooting Series

We now come to the three smallest series in the Safari Press stable, but small can be exceedingly interesting, and we think this is especially true for these last three.

Classics in Sporting Firearms Series

The first book in the Classics in Sporting Firearms Series, *Gun Notes* by Elmer Keith, was also one of the most difficult projects we had ever undertaken because of the editing necessary to make this book readable. For decades Elmer Keith had written a column for *Guns & Ammo* magazine called "Gun Notes." Those in the hunting industry who knew him were well aware that Elmer was both one of the greatest firearms experts of the post World War II era as well as one of the worst gunwriters around. Colorful he was and knowledgeable he was, but poor Elmer could simply not compose a straight English sentence. Jacque's father, Col. Manfred Krause, M.D., was out visiting when we were doing this project. Being knowledgeable about firearms, he helped our editors tremendously by explaining, line by line, what he thought Keith meant. It was such a difficult project that at long last our editors wanted to shout: Write it in plain English! Say what you will about his writings; the public loved him and still does. Two volumes of *Gun Notes* grace our series, and they both have gone through multiple printings. Both volumes came out in limited editions of 500 copies each, and they were both signed by Ted Keith, Elmer's son.

We mentioned earlier that we did not place *Safari Rifles* by Craig Boddington in the Classics in Sporting Firearms Series. However, when Craig wrote a companion rifle book

for hunting in North America entitled *American Hunting Rifles,* we did not make the same mistake. This title became volume two in the Classics in Sporting Firearms Series. Like *Safari Rifles,* we bound *American Hunting Rifles* in leather, this time in red instead of black.

In 1994 we got a call from a certain Robert Braden in Houston who asked if we would meet him. He flew out to California and spent a day in our offices talking about a manuscript he held clutched in his hands. After he was convinced we would do a decent job of publishing his manuscript, he handed it over. He had written the manuscript together with Cyril Adams, the former owner of Atkin, Grant & Lang and one of the finest gentlemen in the gun business in the United States. Thus *Lock, Stock, & Barrel,* volume four in our Sporting Firearms Series, was born. It is one of the finest books ever to explain why British guns are of such phenomenal quality and how they are made with such great care.

When we contracted with Ed Muderlak to produce *Parker Guns, the "Old Reliable"* and announced it to our wholesale accounts in a newsletter, a certain distributor, who shall remain unnamed, told us there were way too many books on Parker guns out there already. Be that as it may, our limited edition sold out within sixty days of the launch of the book, and the title has seen two trade edition printings since. So much for the wisdom of the established book trade! (OK, we admit that we have been guilty of thinking the reverse and being overly optimistic about a book's potential.)

Douglas Tate wrote two books for our Classics in Sporting Firearms Series, and we will admit that his *British Gun Engraving* is one of our favorite Safari Press books of

all time. This visual feast of the finest guns ever made in the United Kingdom is entirely in color and features some of the best gun photography in any book, ever. The irrepressible Marco Nobili wrote *Fine European Gunmakers* as a companion volume to *British Gun Engraving,* and it is the only book Nobili ever wrote entirely in English.

Michael McIntosh & Jan Roosenburg wrote *The Best of Holland & Holland,* a company known for producing extraordinary guns. This book represents our first attempt at doing foldouts, an exceedingly painstaking process in bookmaking. I was intimately involved in the photo shoots for this book, and, consequently, I was in contact with Robert Petersen a lot because so many of Mr. Petersen's magnificent guns are featured in this volume. Little did we suspect at the time that this book would lead us in a direction that would change our lives. Sound dramatic? The events that unfolded *were* dramatic. Because Mr. Petersen and I spoke often on all sorts of subjects, the conversation one day turned to *Sports Afield.* Mr. Petersen had just ceased publication of the magazine that spring of 2002, and he decided that I was the person to take over this venerable old magazine! We spoke often, and Mr. Petersen eventually persuaded me to buy the magazine. I very much doubt this would have happened had I not been involved with him on the Holland & Holland project.

Don Masters wrote two books for our Classics in Sporting Firearms Series, and it is fair to say that both are the most in-depth histories ever published on individual gunmakers. Of course, he had a leg up being a principal and/or owner of both companies for decades. In *The House of Churchill* and

Atkin, Grant & Lang, Don lays out the waxing and waning of some of the best-known names in the United Kingdom gun trade over a period of well over a century. Sadly, we ended up publishing Don's second book posthumously, for he died rather unexpectedly in late 2004.

Forty years ago it was rare for American publishers to seek out African authors, but times change and today having African authors in a publishing company's stable is almost commonplace. So it was with great enthusiasm we welcomed Gregor Woods on board. He wrote *Rifles for Africa,* which is volume twelve in the Classics in Sporting Firearms Series. Gregor Woods, who has spent decades hunting all over southern and eastern Africa, writes for various magazines published in South Africa. His book proved to be tremendously popular, and we have yet to see a secondhand copy of the limited edition of 500 for sale anywhere.

Classics in Hunting at High Altitudes Series

Now we come to our last two series. Safari Press's Hunting at High Altitudes Series has but very few books in it compared with the other series. There just are not that many sheep-hunting manuscripts out there, but the ones we have published are among the finest ever. Moreover, as we write these words in early 2005, we are glad to say that two more great books will be forthcoming soon.

About twenty-five years ago we found a secondhand copy of a book written by Count Ernst Hoyos-Sprinzenstein. The last name couldn't be more Germanic, and, indeed, the book was originally published in 1930 in German. *With a Rifle in Mongolia* is the journal of Hoyos-Sprinzenstein's extraordinary months-long trip for sheep, ibex, and roe deer in Mongolia and China. We had the book translated, and we only ever published 500 copies of it. The negatives were lost shortly thereafter, so it is unlikely that we will print this title again.

Rudolf Sand, a Weatherby award winner and a hunter par excellence, only ever wrote one book in English. We really wanted to publish that book, so when he insisted that we visit him in Denmark to discuss the contract, we immediately agreed. Jacque and I flew to Copenhagen and were entertained in the most charming manner by Rudolf and his wife, Birgit. Their pinewood-paneled house was on a

lake, and there were trophies almost everywhere. Rudolf had an annex built next to his house for his African heads and even that room was overflowing. His book, *Those Were the Days,* became volume two in our Classics in Hunting at High Altitudes Series. This book tells of international sheep and ibex hunting directly after World War II and is one of the most honest and truthful accounts written by a sheep hunter. Our only regret is that we could not get Rudolf to include the story of a tremendous bighorn he had shot in Canada. Apparently, the trophy was stolen en route back to Denmark, and because the head was hanging in another hunter's trophy room, Rudolf would not write about it, despite our pleadings. Rudolf even went so far as to return to Montana to shoot a sheep in the unlimited area, thus completing his collection. This story he did include in the book.

It is hard to describe Rashid Jamsheed's sheep hunting career without superlatives. James Mellon once told me that Jamsheed's sheep collection was the finest that he had ever seen, and even Prince Abdorreza admitted to us that some of Jamsheed's heads from Iran were bigger than his own. Therefore, when we realized that Rashid had a manuscript, we jumped on the chance to publish it. *Memories of a Sheep Hunter* became volume three in the series, and its remarkable pictures are a visual treat for sheep hunters everywhere. I was fortunate enough to see Rashid's trophy room in person as well as all eleven heads that represent sheep-hunting records. The only thing better than the room was his wife Norma's cooking, who despite being a native-born American prepared the best Persian rice dishes I had ever eaten!

Jesús Yurén has written several books in Spanish that were published in Mexico. His only English-language book is *Song of the Summits,* which follows his journeys along the summits and canyons throughout the world for sheep, ibex, and other members of the Caprini tribe. Other people have shot sheep and wild goats, but Jesús Yurén has shot *a lot* of sheep and goats. And when we say a lot , we do mean a great many. He is one of the most dedicated mountain hunters of all time.

Finally, this seems an appropriate place to mention one book that is not part of our series but needs to be identified for collectors. Some years back Ricardo Medem published his book *Argali* simultaneously in English and Spanish. The

book was published in Madrid, and Ricardo and I talked about Safari Press distributing it in the United States. Through a misunderstanding at the bindery in Spain, the English edition was bound in dark blue ribbed cloth with a Safari Press logo on the spine. When the books arrived here in the United States, we saw this and, although very flattered, we did not want to have our trademark logo used on books we did not publish. So Ricardo Medem, ever the gentleman, agreed to have the books rebound by a U.S. bindery in green cloth without the Safari Press logo. A few copies of the dark blue binding were sent from Spain to reviewers here in the United States. Although we managed to retrieve some of them, we estimate that fewer than a dozen copies are still out there somewhere. Quite easily this binding of *Argali* is the rarest of all "Safari Press" books!

Classics in Wingshooting Series

Finally we have the Classics in Wingshooting Series, which has but three books in it so far. Richard Grozik's *Birdhunter,* volume one in this series, is a celebration of wild birds, fine guns, and staunch dogs. His essays are a joy to read. We previously mentioned Robert Braden's first book. His second one entitled *As I Look Back* is equally as interesting. Regaling us with bird-hunting tales from the Outer Hebrides to the foothills of the Himalayas (have you ever heard of snipe shooting from an elephant's back?), this to us is a joyous series of bird-hunting vignettes that will be hard to equal for the new generation of wingshooting writers. Finally we have *When Ducks Were Plenty* by Ed Muderlak, who has expertly compiled articles from long-forgotten magazines on the heyday of duck hunting in North America. If the articles are to be believed, the sky in those days remained black with the number of birds flying overhead.

This concludes our introduction to the various hunting series produced by Safari Press. We hope this information is of help to you in collecting our fine, limited-edition books.

Ludo Wurfbain, *Publisher*

Gun Notes*

Elmer Keith's *Guns & Ammo* Articles of the 1960s

by Elmer Keith

Well-known gunwriter Elmer Keith wrote a monthly column for *Guns & Ammo* magazine for three decades entitled "Gun Notes." Keith was a master storyteller as well as a most observant gun expert. He was one of the country's best-known experts on big-bore calibers, and these books have a wealth of information based on his lifelong experience with just about every imaginable sporting firearm. Also included are letters from Elmer Keith to Truman Fowler, publisher of Keith's *Safari* book, and correspondence from Fowler (a well-known big-bore advocate) to Jack O'Connor, who took exception to much of what Keith and Fowler recommended. This is highly entertaining reading—the pages of the correspondence literally sizzle under your fingertips! Illustrated with photos from the *Guns & Ammo* files.

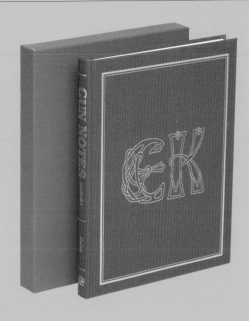

Volume I This book contains the best of his articles from 1961 until the late 1970s and is entirely devoted to pistols, revolvers, bolt action and double rifles, shotguns, ammunition, loads, bullets, and accessories. Foreword by Ross Seyfried. This is **volume one** in Safari Press's **Classics in Sporting Firearms Series.** 1995 Long Beach, 219pp, b&w photos, 8.5x11, hardcover. Limited edition of 500 numbered, and slipcased copies signed by son Ted Keith. .... Original Issue Price $75.00

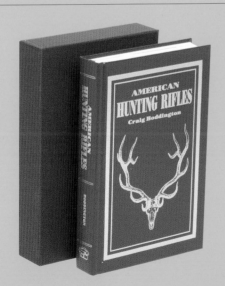

American Hunting Rifles*

Their Application in the Field for Practical Shooting, with Notes on Handguns and Shotguns

by Craig Boddington

A companion volume to Boddington's highly acclaimed *Safari Rifles*, this comprehensive book covers all the hunting rifles and calibers that are needed for North America's diverse game. From the great bears of the Arctic to the diminutive javelina of the Southwest deserts, America's game calls for a large variety of calibers, and Boddington covers them all, in the thorough, clear, and concise manner that we have come to expect of him. This incredible work will be a guide to all North American hunters, whether you shoot whitetails on the East Coast or elk in the Rocky Mountains. It covers literally all North American big game and all imaginable rifles, calibers, and shooting gear. This book also contains a detailed twenty-four-page index and outfitter recommendations on rifles and calibers. Foreword by Robert Elman. This is **volume two** in Safari Press's **Classics in Sporting Firearms Series.** 1995 Long Beach, 446pp, photos, 6.25x9.25, leather bound. Limited edition of 500 signed, numbered, and slipcased copies. .... Original Issue Price $85.00

*SOLD OUT. LISTS ORIGINAL ISSUE PRICE.

Frank A. Pachmayr

America's Master Gunsmith and His Guns

by John Lachuk

This is the colorful biography of Frank A. Pachmayr, America's own gunsmith emeritus. Anybody who is at all interested in American firearms will know of Frank Pachmayr. Born in Germany, Pachmayr immigrated with his family to the United States and settled in the Los Angeles area. He grew up under the thorough tutelage of his stern father, August, a towering figure who achieved the stature of Master Gunsmith in his native country. Upon maturity, with zero assets, Frank embarked upon an independent gunsmithing career at the very outset of the Great Depression. By dint of stubborn courage and hard work, he scratched his way to wealth and international prominence. Pachmayr is conceded to be the first to improve the U.S. Military Model 1911A1/Colt Government Model into today's most popular combat/target pistol. He originated the modern rubber recoil pads and neoprene pistol grips that still bear his name. He created some of the most valuable and beautifully engraved rifles and shotguns ever seen. Pachmayr made major contributions to America's armaments through two major wars, and he pioneered research into many of today's most modern weapons' systems. He was and is a major contributor to wildlife preservation. Officially endorsed by Pachmayr, this book is filled with historical photos as well as photos of the fabulous Pachmayr guns. Introduction by Col. Charles Askins. This is **volume three** in Safari Press's **Classics in Sporting Firearms Series**. 1995 Long Beach, 302pp, photos in b&w and color, 7x10, hardcover. Limited edition of 500 signed, numbered, and slipcased copies. $85.00

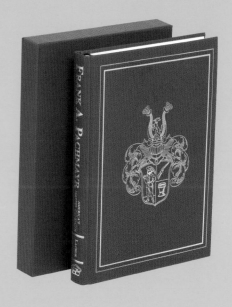

Lock, Stock, & Barrel

Making an English Shotgun and Shooting with Consistency

by Cyril S. Adams & Robert S. Braden

Cyril Adams and Robert Braden are unanimous in their preference for an English-made shotgun over all other makes, and their book gives the best description ever of the process of making a best-grade English gun from a lump of steel and a walnut tree trunk to the ultimate product: the lock, stock, and barrel. The reader will completely understand what goes into such a gun and why they are so expensive. The book also contains practical advice on consistent field shooting with a double gun; an extensive bibliography; and tips on choke, shot pattern, shooting distance, and other technical aspects, which is why this book was selected as one of the ten best sporting books of 1996 by *Sports Afield!** Foreword by Bob Brister. This is **volume four** in Safari Press's **Classics in Sporting Firearms Series**. 1996 Long Beach, 198pp, photos, 6x9, hardcover. Limited edition of 500 signed, numbered, and slipcased copies. $60.00

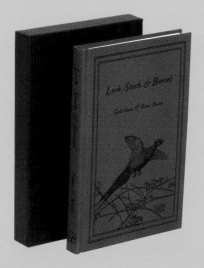

*This happened long before the owners of Safari Press acquired *Sports Afield!*

Birmingham Gunmakers*

A Complete Overview of the Birmingham Gun Trade and Its History
as well as a Listing of the Birmingham Gunmakers

by Douglas Tate

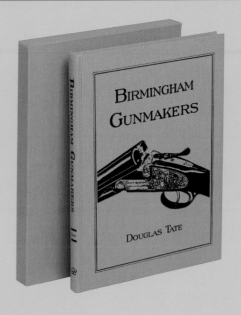

Birmingham Gunmakers is the most complete work ever published on the famous British gunmakers of Birmingham. Tate gives a thorough overview of the origins of the Birmingham gun trade as well as a history of how the city came to the foreground as one of the sporting-gun manufacturing centers of the world. He covers the well-known makers as well as the obscure—those who have long since ceased production and vanished into the mists of time. Birmingham has produced some of the most famous names in the world of sporting guns such as W. W. Greener, William Powell, Westley Richards, and many others. All these are thoroughly covered, and the book is illustrated with some of the finest examples of their craftsmanship. The Birmingham Gun Barrel Proof House, buying and evaluating a Birmingham gun, and a glossary of gunmaker terms are also included. An invaluable book for anyone interested in fine sporting arms. This is **volume five** in Safari Press's **Classics in Sporting Firearms Series.** 1997 Long Beach, 190pp plus 32pp of color photos, b&w photos, 8.5x11, hardcover. Limited edition of 500 signed, numbered, and slipcased copies. .... Original Issue Price $80.00

Gun Notes

Elmer Keith's *Guns & Ammo* Articles of the 1970s and 1980s

by Elmer Keith

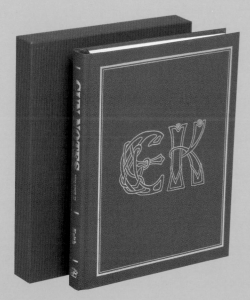

Well-known gunwriter Elmer Keith wrote a monthly column for *Guns & Ammo* magazine for three decades entitled "Gun Notes." Keith was a master storyteller as well as a most observant gun expert. He was one of the country's best-known experts on big-bore calibers, and these books have a wealth of information based on his lifelong experience with just about every imaginable sporting firearm. Also included are letters from Elmer Keith to Truman Fowler, publisher of Keith's *Safari* book, and correspondence from Fowler (a well-known big-bore advocate) to Jack O'Connor, who took exception to much of what Keith and Fowler recommended. This is highly entertaining reading—the pages of the correspondence literally sizzle under your fingertips! Illustrated with photos from the *Guns & Ammo* files.

Volume II In this second volume, excerpts from the years 1971 through 1980 are published. As in the previous volume, his writings reek of gun oil, saddle leather, gunpowder, and campfires as well as pistols, revolvers, bolt action and double rifles, shotguns, ammunition, loads, bullets, and numerous accessories. Foreword by Craig Boddington. This is **volume six** in Safari Press's **Classics in Sporting Firearms Series.** 1996 Long Beach, 292pp, b&w photos, 8.5x11, hardcover. Limited edition of 500 numbered, slipcased copies, signed by son Ted Keith. $75.00

Parker Guns, the "Old Reliable"*

by Ed Muderlak

The Parker Gun Company is a never-ending source of interest for collectors of American shotguns. Unlike most gunwriters, Ed Muderlak has done a remarkable job doing original research instead of repeating the same (and often mistaken) information of others. The interesting results will shock you as they reverse the conventional wisdom that's been followed for years. Muderlak takes a refreshing look at the small beginnings, the golden years, and the ultimate decline of what is, no doubt, the most famous of all American shotgun manufacturers. Profusely illustrated with dozens of color photos of Parker guns as well as historical photos in black and white, this well-written and concise text also includes a thorough appendix that lists grades, patents, gun weights, serial numbers, and many other specifications for the Parker enthusiast. Foreword by Herschel Chadick. This is **volume seven** in Safari Press's **Classics in Sporting Firearms Series.** 1997 Long Beach, 270pp plus 44pp of color photos, 8.5x11, hardcover. Limited edition of 500 signed, numbered, and slipcased copies. .... Original Issue Price $85.00

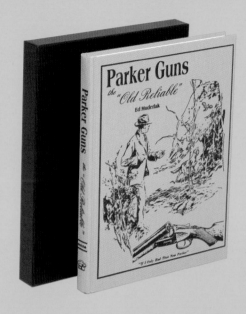

British Gun Engraving*

by Douglas Tate

Douglas Tate and master photographer David Grant bring us the most opulent examples of British gun engraving in existence from the greatest private collections in Europe and the United States. This book traces the traditions of British gun engraving from the end of the eighteenth century to today. This fine production chronicles Celtic engraving as practiced chiefly by Scottish makers, the influence of the Arts and Crafts movement, and the significance the Indian maharajahs had on British gun ornamentation. David Grant's superb photographic plates illustrate every aspect of British gun engraving. This is **volume eight** in Safari Press's **Classics in Sporting Firearms Series.** 2000 Long Beach, 274pp, 300 color photos, 10.5x8.5, hardcover. Limited edition of 500 signed, numbered, and slipcased copies. .... Original Issue Price $80.00

Fine European Gunmakers*

Best Continental European Gunmakers & Engravers

by Marco E. Nobili

Hundreds of books have been published about the British gun trade, but English writers and publishers have largely ignored the European makers of fine guns until now. Marco Nobili's new work exhibits the skills of the best craftsmen from continental Europe, and the author brings to life in words and pictures their finest sporting guns. The book covers the histories of the individual firms and looks at the guns they currently build, tracing the developments of their most influential models. Depicted with profuse color photos, *Fine European Gunmakers* showcases the best guns ever made in Europe. All the greatest names are here, including Piotti, Beretta, Krieghoff, Connecticut Shotgun, Perazzi, Hartmann & Weiss, Peter Hofer, Gamba, Fanzoj, Lebeau & Courally, Fabbri, and many others. This exciting and valuable new reference work, profusely illustrated in color, will be an important addition to the bookshelf of any serious collector, or anyone who is simply enamored of fine sporting guns. This is **volume nine** in Safari Press's **Classics in Sporting Firearms Series.** 2002 Long Beach, 301pp, color and b&w photos, 10.5x8.5, hardcover. Limited edition of 500 signed, numbered, and slipcased copies. .... Original Issue Price ... $85.00

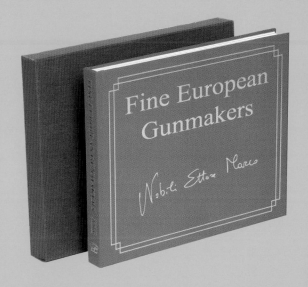

The Best of Holland & Holland*

England's Premier Gunmaker

by Michael McIntosh and Jan Roosenburg

Holland & Holland has had a long history of not only building London's "best" guns but also providing superior guns—the ultimate gun in finish, engraving, and embellishment. From the days of old in which a maharajah would order 200 fancifully engraved H&H shotguns for his guests to use at his duck shoot to recent times with elaborately decorated sets depicting such diverse subjects as the Apollo 11 moon landing or the history of the British Empire, all the guns produced by H&H represent the zenith in the art and craft of gunmaking and engraving. In this book master gunwriter and acknowledged English gun expert Michael McIntosh and former H&H director Jan Roosenburg describe and identify the finest products ever produced by H&H and, many would argue, by any gun company on earth. From a dainty and elegant .410 shotgun with gold relief engraving of scenes from Greek and Roman antiquity to a massive .700 Nitro Express double rifle, some of the most expensive and opulent guns ever produced on earth parade through these pages. An overview of the Products of Excellence Series is given as well as a description and history of these special H&H guns. Never before have so many superlative guns from H&H—or any other maker for that matter—been displayed in one book. Many photos shown are firearms from private collections, which cannot be seen publicly anywhere except in this book. In addition, the authors provide many interesting details and a thorough history of H&H. This is **volume ten** in Safari Press's **Classics in Sporting Firearms Series.** 2003 Long Beach, 298pp, color and b&w photos, 10.5x8.5, hardcover. Limited edition of 500 signed, numbered, and slipcased copies. .... Original Issue Price ... $125.00

The House of Churchill*

by Don Masters

The world-renowned Churchill Gunmakers was formed in 1891 and is one of the best known of all English gunmakers. The reader will find in these pages the complete history as well as wonderfully entertaining anecdotes of the Churchill family and its colorful gunmaking members, including Edwin J. Churchill, who established the company, and Robert Churchill, who became known as an international gunmaker and ballistics expert. The history of the company and its guns is also thoroughly analyzed. There is detailed information on the glory years, the famous Churchill XXV gun, which was advocated by Robert Churchill but had its detractors, the difficult pre-World War II years, the Atkin, Grant, & Lang years, and the age of conglomerates. It contains serial numbers and dates of manufacture of its guns from 1891 forward, price lists from 1895 onward, a complete listing of all craftsmen employed at the company, as well as the prices realized at the famous Dallas auction where the "last" production guns were sold. In addition it includes much information on the London and Birmingham Proof Houses and the general administration of the gun trade. This massive work is well illustrated with hundreds of color and black and white photos, period brochures, and gun labels, and it includes dozens of charts, tables, appendixes, and a detailed index. This is **volume eleven** in Safari Press's **Classics in Sporting Firearms Series.** 2002 Long Beach, 531pp, profuse color and b&w photos, 8.5x11, hardcover. Limited edition of 500 signed, numbered, and slipcased copies. .... Original Issue Price $95.00

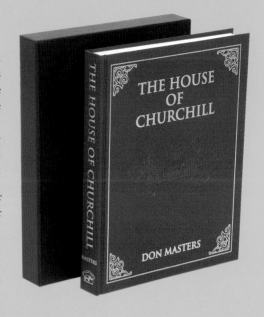

Rifles for Africa*

Practical Advice on Rifles and Ammunition for an African Safari

by Gregor Woods

Gregor Woods is one of the most experienced hunters today on the African continent, having shot game with everything from small centerfire .22 calibers right up to some of the most powerful cartridges available. In this milestone book, he gives the reader his experiences and conclusions based upon forty years of hunting most of the game animals of the Dark Continent. Based in Durban, South Africa, he has made dozens of safaris to the classic African game fields of Zimbabwe, Tanzania, Namibia, Botswana, and South Africa, where he has had numerous experiences with dangerous game as well as with the dozens of varieties of antelope. Readers of *Magnum* magazine will recognize his name as the author of numerous articles in which his no-nonsense, practical bent shines. This latest work is invaluable to the person who seeks advice and information on what rifles, calibers, and bullets work on African big game, be they the largest land mammals on earth or an antelope barely weighing in at twenty pounds. The reader will be much enlightened by what Woods considers to be minimum standards for bullet performance, sights, and rifle functioning. Foreword by Brian Marsh. This is **volume twelve** in Safari Press's **Classics in Sporting Firearms Series.** 2002 Long Beach, 465pp, 273 b&w photos, 6x9, hardcover. Limited edition of 500 signed, numbered, and slipcased copies. .... Original Issue Price $85.00

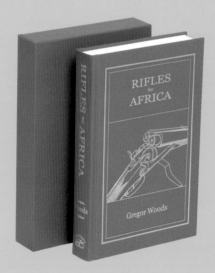

Rifles and Cartridges for Large Game*

From Deer to Bear—Advice on the Choice of a Rifle

by Layne Simpson

Layne Simpson, who has been field editor for *Shooting Times* magazine for twenty years, draws from his hunting experiences on five continents to tell you what rifles, cartridges, bullets, loads, and scopes are best for various applications. Developer of the popular 7mm STW cartridge, Simpson has taken big game with rifle cartridges ranging in power from the .220 Swift to the .460 Weatherby Magnum, and he pulls no punches when describing their effectiveness in the field. A sample of the thirty-one chapters includes: "The Woods Rifle," "The Mountain Rifle," "Medicine For Dangerous Game," "The Custom Rifle," "The Beanfield Rifle," and "The Saddle Rifle." If you are interested in the equipment needed to successfully hunt white-tailed deer, pronghorn antelope, elk, mule deer, caribou, black bear, moose, Alaska brown bear, Cape buffalo, African lion, or any other big-game animal, this book is a must. *Rifles and Cartridges for Large Game* has one hundred color photos and is an oversize book. Foreword by Ed Weatherby. This is **volume thirteen** in Safari Press's **Classics in Sporting Firearms Series.** 2003 Long Beach, 325pp, profuse color photos, 8.5x11, hardcover. Limited edition of 500 signed, numbered, and slipcased copies. ..... Original Issue Price $65.00

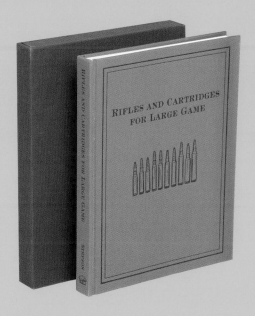

Atkin, Grant & Lang

Don Masters

Don Masters has been a leading figure in the British gunmaking business for decades. His previous book on the Churchill gun company received universal praise. Well known for his accurate and meticulous research, Masters has undertaken the detailed history of the gunmakers that would eventually be known as Atkin, Grant & Lang. But this book is more than a simple history of the firms of Henry Atkin, established in 1877, Stephen Grant, founded in 1867, and Joseph Lang, formed in 1825. It is also the history of their several relatives making guns under their own names. In addition, many other companies whose histories are intertwined with Atkin, Grant & Lang are covered: Hussey, Grant & Woodward, Lancaster, Watson, Harrison, Beesley, Hellis, and Wright. Each company had a long, successful run in making double guns, mainly shotguns. Until World War I, the British sporting gun reigned supreme, but after that cataclysmic war, the fortunes of the industry changed drastically and after World War II went into a severe decline. All three firms, however, managed to hold on until eventually they were merged to form the famous trio. In the pages of this book you can learn all the details of the gunmakers: dates, premises, main employees, rises and declines in sales fortunes, as well as the many interesting historical anecdotes and insights we have come to expect from Don Masters. This reference work contains hundreds of photos in black and white and color, written by a man who has done more research into the extensive archives of all these gunmakers than any other person. This is **volume fourteen** in Safari Press's **Classics in Sporting Firearms Series**. 2005 Long Beach, 316pp, color and b&w photos, 8.5x11, hardcover. Limited edition of 500 signed, numbered, and slipcased copies. ..... Original Issue Price $100.00

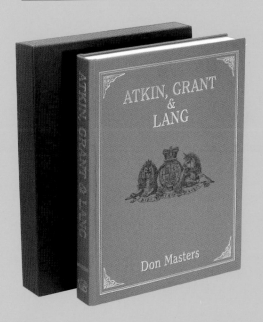

Classics in Hunting at High Altitudes Series

THE SAFARI PRESS LIMITED EDITION COLLECTION

With a Rifle in Mongolia*

In the Altai and the Tian Shan

by Count Ernst Hoyos-Sprinzenstein

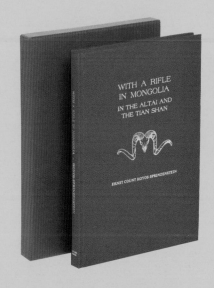

This is the translation of Hoyos-Sprinzenstein's account of his 1911 hunting expedition into Central Asia. Count Hoyos-Sprinzenstein hunted extensively for Altai argali and ibex in Mongolia and China. He shot about as many sheep as any early hunter (he obtained close to three dozen sheep and ibex!). Among his trophies were some of the biggest heads obtained to that date. While this title is predominately on sheep and ibex, there are also snow leopard and wapiti (maral) included. This is **volume one** in Safari Press's **Classics in Hunting at High Altitudes Series.** 1986 Long Beach, 144pp, 64 photos, endpaper maps, 6.5x9.5, hardcover. Limited edition of 500 signed, numbered, and slipcased copies. .... Original Issue Price $85.00

When we brought out this title, we stated that "no other edition would ever be issued."

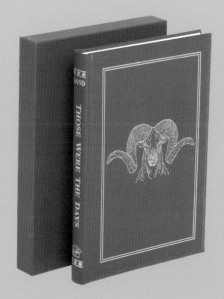

Those Were the Days*

Thirty Years of Hunting the Wild Sheep and Goats of the World

by Rudolf Sand

For over thirty years, Rudolf Sand scaled the pinnacles of Asia, Africa, and America in his search for every species of wild goat and sheep. He traveled from the deserts of North America to the mountains of British Columbia, the Tibetan plateau to the Gobi Desert, and the Afghan Pamirs to the Kamchatka Peninsula. He shot over twenty-four varieties of sheep and twenty varieties of goat—a virtual lifetime of hunting. Clearly, this book is by far the most comprehensive on hunting sheep and goats by any one author. This luxury edition includes cover stamping, beveled edges, the finest grade cloth, and acid-free paper—a masterpiece of fine bookcrafting. Introduction by James Mellon. This is **volume two** in Safari Press's **Classics in Hunting at High Altitudes Series.** 1992 Long Beach, 294 pages, color and b&w photos, 7x10, hardcover. Limited edition of 1,000 signed, numbered, and slipcased copies. .... Original Issue Price $90.00

*SOLD OUT. LISTS ORIGINAL ISSUE PRICE.

Memories of a Sheep Hunter*

by Rashid Jamsheed

Living legend and holder of eleven sheep-hunting records, Rashid Jamsheed tells an exciting story of obtaining world-record heads from his native Iran, from around the world, and from the United States where he procured a Grand Slam of North American sheep. Jamsheed's trophies are as varied and impressive as the list of countries in which he has hunted. In Central Asia he obtained heads of Altai argali, Gobi argali, and Marco Polo argali—all of which are outstanding trophy quality due to his refusal to compromise his standards. For his Marco Polo sheep, he traveled three times to Asia and spent a combined ninety days before he connected with the ram of his dreams, an extraordinary 67-incher! He also tells of shooting some of the best markhor trophies ever—two of the heads reaching 60 inches—with his Sulaiman markhor holding the world record! He has hunted every mountain range in Pakistan and Afghanistan in order to collect various markhor subspecies, and he has some of the biggest ibex heads ever taken. Foreword by Stanley T. Escudero, and introduction by Carlo Caldesi. This is **volume three** in Safari Press's **Classics in Hunting at High Altitudes Series.** 1996 Long Beach, 333pp, 103 color and b&w photos, 8.5x11, hardcover. Limited edition of 500 signed, numbered, and slipcased copies. ....^{Original Issue Price}.... $125.00

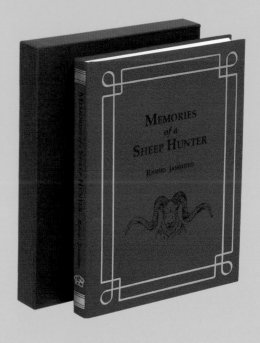

Song of the Summits

Memoirs from the High Country

by Jesús Yurén

A master of sheep and ibex hunting, Yurén has hunted on most mountains of the earth, from Alaska and Mexico to China, Mongolia, and Russia. Accumulating a North American Grand Slam as well as a Super Slam of sheep, he has hunted just about every variety of wild sheep and goat in the world. Starting in 1972 with a desert bighorn, he continued for Rocky Mountain, Dall, and Stone sheep. In Asia he climbed after Marco Polo, Altai, Gansu, Gobi, Littledale, Hume, Karaganda, Tibetan, and other argalis as well as various Asian and European ibex. He also added to his bag of experiences blue sheep, Himalayan tahr, Nubian ibex, and Barbary sheep as well as chamois and Spanish ibex, all of which he hunted in their native habitat. Amusing and humorous as well as exciting, Yurén's book reveals the tremendous physical strength and great mental fortitude that is required for mountain hunting. Yurén's modesty, jovial spirit, and sense of humor make him a very likable author; his wealth of experience makes him a fascinating one. Artwork by Luís Yurén, and two forewords: one by Robin Hurt and one by Ricardo Medem. This is **volume four** in Safari Press's **Classics in Hunting at High Altitudes Series.** 2003 Long Beach, 359pp, b&w photos, 7x10, hardcover. Limited edition of 1,000 signed, numbered, and slipcased copies. $75.00

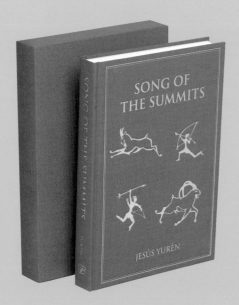

The Safari Press warehouse in Huntington Beach, California

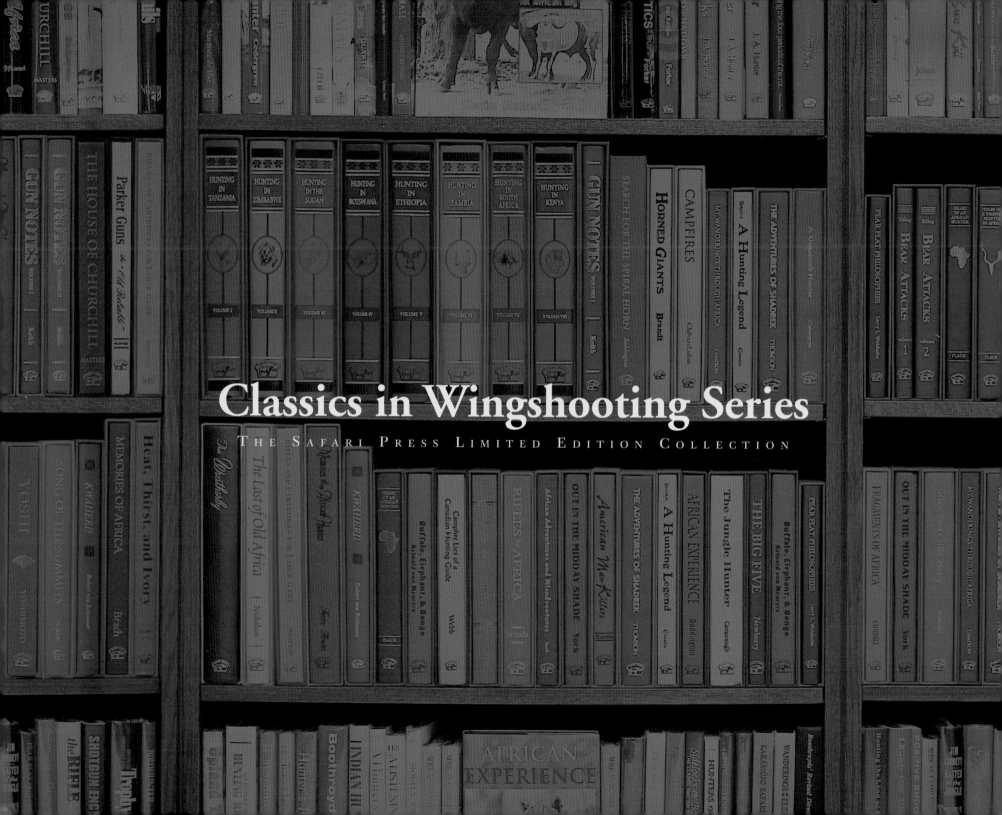

Classics in Wingshooting Series

The Safari Press Limited Edition Collection

Birdhunter*

A Celebration of Wild Birds, Fine Guns, and Staunch Dogs

by Richard S. Grozik

Grozik says in his introduction, "Few things in life are as sacred to me as a well-balanced game gun, a biddable bird dog, and an understanding spouse. . . . Selecting the perfect game gun, like marrying the ideal mate, has renewed my faith in miracles." Second only to his search for a perfect game gun is his desire to own just one more good bird dog. His gun dog must exhibit blind obedience to its woefully untrained master, must point stylishly, hold steady to wing and shot, and tenderly retrieve game birds while its master fills its ears with empty threats and all manner of confusing commands. Grozik, humorously, never admits to having any other type of dog. If any of this strikes a familiar chord, this book is for you. You may not find the solution to all your birdhunting afflictions in this book, but you can take solace in knowing there are others who share your sentiment, if not your predicament. This lively, well-written book is an entertaining salute to the closeness between man and his dog, man and his gun, and man and the great outdoors. Artwork by Herb Booth, and foreword by Dan Busse. This is **volume one** in Safari Press's **Classics in Wingshooting Series.** 1997 Long Beach, 162pp, 6x9, hardcover. Limited edition of 500 signed, numbered, and slipcased copies. ...._{Original Issue Price}... $60.00

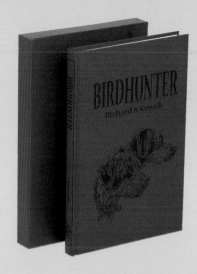

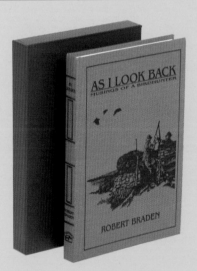

As I Look Back

Musings of a Birdhunter

by Robert Braden

Those who have read *Lock, Stock, & Barrel* already know that Robert Braden is a fanatic birdhunter and connoisseur of English side-by-side guns. In his last book, Robert Braden shares his recollections of bird hunting around the world. Join Braden and his guests at their yearly hunt in Mexico; follow along with Braden and his partner Cyril Adams as they shoot birds from the backs of elephants in India; go with Braden to a remote island in the United Kingdom hunting for exotic and unusual birds; and come back home with Braden as he stakes out the banks of his home-state river for duck. These are only a few of the fascinating vignettes that reveal the funny, interesting, and sometimes sad tales of Braden's marvelous birdhunting career. This refreshing and interesting book is from a writer with vast experience. Artwork by Jeff Jackson. This is **volume two** in Safari Press's **Classics in Wingshooting Series.** 1999 Long Beach, 178pp, 6x9, hardcover. Limited edition of 500 signed, numbered, and slipcased copies.................... $50.00

* SOLD OUT. LISTS ORIGINAL ISSUE PRICE.

When Ducks Were Plenty

The Golden Age of Duck Hunting. A Pictorial and Written Anthology of the Origins, History, Impact, and Prospects of the Grand Passage of Waterfowl in America Describing the Haunts, Habits, and Methods of Shooting All Manner of Wildfowl in Their Diverse Locations, from the 1840s to about 1920

edited by Ed Muderlak

Ed Muderlak has gathered some fifty-odd stories from thousands of journals and hundreds of books that are among the best ever written on the early duck-hunting days of this country. The book is jam-packed with exciting waterfowling stories from the golden age of waterfowling—beginning with Frank Forester's tale of shooting rail on the Delaware River in the 1840s to William Hazelton's description of bagging mallards in flooded timber along the Illinois River in 1920. Some of the stories are outrageously exaggerated, but the exaggeration is just part of what makes this book such fun reading. Extensively annotated by the editor to put the stories in perspective, this book gives a unique view of our waterfowling history as well as being an exceptionally fine read. Foreword by "Gaucho" (pseudonym of Capt. Arthur W. du Bray). This is **volume three** in Safari Press's **Classics in Wingshooting Series**. 2000 Long Beach, 390pp, illustrated with period photos and drawings, 6x9, hardcover. Limited edition of 500 signed, numbered, and slipcased copies. $60.00

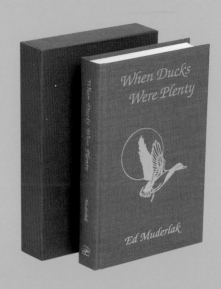

Convention preparations